48

DAYS

TO THE WORK

YOU LOVE

DAN MILLER

48
DAYS
TO THE WORK
YOU LOVE

PUBLISHING GROUP
Nashville, Tennessee

Contents

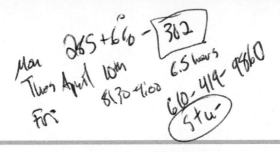

Author's Note

The workplace has continued to be ravaged by changes since the first edition of *48 Days to the Work You Love*. We have seen the collapse of major financial institutions, auto manufacturers, real estate companies, and thousands of smaller companies around the world. But with those changes we've also seen a new phenomenon unfolding. Forced to look for work, many people have experienced a wake-up call, realizing they could choose or create work that is more than just a paycheck. They have discovered the thrill of work that blends their strongest talents, their personality traits, and their dreams and passions.

Yes, many of the old work models are being eliminated, never to return again. But no, there are not fewer opportunities; they just look different. These dramatic changes are creating new and exciting opportunities that would not have even been possible four or five years ago. The world has become flattened—meaning you can apply for positions with organizations that are not even in the same country where you choose to live. The chances of having a "job" with a guaranteed salary and benefits are diminishing, but it's never been easier to define new work models that allow for increased time, freedom, and income.

And no, the process for finding work that "fits" and is the application of our "calling" has not changed. As outlined in the original *48 Days to the Work You Love,* I believe that 85 percent of the process of determining the right career direction comes from looking inward—15 percent is the application to fitting work. That process of looking inward has not changed. It's still a proven process of finding your unique talents, creating a clear focus, and then finding—or creating—the appropriate application for meaningful, fulfilling, purposeful, and profitable work.

Thus, with this revised edition we will look at the changing trends and the impact of recent changes on the workplace. The process of finding work that "fits" is not a one-time event. Whether you are eighteen or sixty-eight, fulfilling work requires an ongoing understanding of who we are and who we are becoming. Each transition point in life (even if unexpected and unwelcomed) gives us a fresh opportunity to realign our daily activities in order to embrace our continued maturity and our ability to contribute effectively.

I asked the 48 Days readers and listeners for suggestions for this revised edition. I received more than 165,000 words—more than two entire books if they were all included. The suggestions were insightful and many have been included in what you are about to read. (Many more are included in our additional resources at www.48Days.com/worksheets.) You'll see lots of real-life questions and solutions regarding the challenges and opportunities in today's world. Thank you so much to all of you who so willingly shared from your own life experience.

Prepare for the new normal.

Foreword

In my work with those who are struggling financially, I hear an often repeated theme—the struggle to make fatiguing work produce adequate income. As you will see from the real testimonials in this book, *48 Days to the Work You Love* continues to be a popular resource for changing that equation. While it is not a book about finances, the natural result of having a clear understanding of Skills and Abilities, Personality Tendencies, and Passions is to match those with work that is fulfilling, meaningful—*and profitable.*

Dan's insight and actual hands-on implementation of discovering and developing a calling has influenced thousands of lives, including mine and many of my team members. You see, implementation is the key. In the last few years I have been very inspired to be "wild at heart" and to have a "purpose-driven life" and am a huge fan of those culture-impacting books (by John Eldredge and Rick Warren, respectively). I am even more excited by *48 Days to the Work You Love* because it puts clothes on the concepts. You may be like me; I sometimes need someone to help me put the concepts into action. Knowledge without action is personified in the overeducated broke and broken who wander listlessly among us.

The following pages lead you to implement a step-by-step plan to show the world your purpose and your heart in a way that is most satisfying. It is satisfying not because you will never face adversity or make mistakes in the process nor because your career will zoom ahead and never falter. You will fall, you will err, and your career will not take a perfect path. No, this material is satisfying and life-changing because you will have the tools to discover a key part of the plan God has for your life. This material is satisfying because when you begin discovering and *implementing* this plan, you will have a sense of God-given power that will propel you through adversity and errors. This new God-given power will give you the energy to recognize that even wrong turns can benefit the end result.

In the last several years, while meeting and spending time with people who have become inordinately successful, I have observed several common traits among them. Two of those traits stand out. One is they have a calling, which they have discovered and are implementing. The other is they have made mountains of mistakes in the process of becoming "successful." The gleaming mountain of success is actually a pile of trash—a pile of the mistakes we have made. The difference between the successful and the troubled is not error-free living; it is that by discovering and implementing a life calling, the successful stand on their pile of trash while the troubled sit under theirs.

Most of us spend too much of our lives in paralyzing fear, shame, guilt, and dread when it comes to our work. Work has become the daily grind instead of the great adventure it should be. The beauty of this material is that as you implement it, you will gradually diminish your negative emotions and move into a thriving work life. As someone who lives this material every day, I know you will still experience doubt, fear, and mistakes. However, by finding and functioning in your calling, you will increasingly grow in confidence that you were put here to win in spite of those things, not without them.

I am excited for you because by opening these next few pages you are lighting a fire. The wood may be old and wet, but it has the capacity to become a raging bonfire! This is a book about implementation, *so do it!*

Dave Ramsey
Nationally Syndicated Radio Host

Introduction

Very early in life we begin to determine what we want to be when we grow up. You may remember the childhood nursery rhyme: "Rich Man, Poor Man, Beggar Man, Thief, Doctor, Lawyer, Merchant, Chief." We add other titles to that and begin to imagine the life as a Firefighter, Teacher, Entrepreneur, or Dentist. But as we begin school and start to grow up, there is a subtle yet significant transition from "Who do I want to be?" to "What am I going to do?" We are defined and valued in America by what we do. Unfortunately, the path to *doing* something often bypasses the basic questions about *being* something.

This book will address "who do you want to be" as the starting point for "what do you want to do." The more you know yourself the more confidence you can have about doing work that fits you. And the more you know about yourself, the more you recognize the freedom you have in choosing work that is meaningful, purposeful, and profitable.

Having the freedom to choose our work means we can choose from the popular models—employee, independent contractor, consultant, contingency worker, freelancer, temp, entrepreneur, self-employed, electronic immigrant worker, and more. Interestingly, the theory behind most governmental systems is that "the people" do not want freedom. They want guaranteed paychecks, medical benefits, workers' compensation, fringe benefits, and a retirement plan. And in exchange for those outcomes, people give up the freedom to find or create work that is a blend of their talents, dreams,

1

and spiritual calling. For many people, work has become nothing more than a paycheck and benefits. It is an accepted stance to hate our jobs and to belittle the boss and the company, while patting ourselves on the back for being "responsible providers" for ourselves and families. Give up your freedom and you'll have two cars in the garage, a fine house, a nice vacation once a year, and you will no longer have to suffer the agony of choice.

But wait a minute. Isn't that what growing up is all about? Doesn't every responsible person forget about dreams and passions in exchange for getting a paycheck? Absolutely not! Let me assure you that it doesn't need to be this way at all. Each of us, no matter what age we are or what kind of work we're doing now, can learn to bring the same excitement to our work that we experienced as a child at play. I believe each of us can pursue work that is a reflection of our best selves—a true application of our calling in life.

Recognizing the freedom we have to choose our work also brings with it the responsibility to accept the results of our work. The sense of fulfillment our work brings, the paycheck provided, and the assurance that our work is making the world a better place are all ours to choose. No one is trapped in today's workplace. We get to choose.

For many of you, *48 Days to the Work You Love* will present a process of waking up the dreams, passions, and visions you had as a child. For many people, the mergers, downsizing, firing, forced retirement, and other forms of unexpected change in the workplace in the last few years have served as a clarion wake-up call for dreams that had gone dormant. Many people were given the opportunity to take a fresh look at "Who am I and why am I here?" The moment you express a desire for something more than repetitive, meaningless work, something more than simply punching the clock, the moment you realize that meaningful, purposeful, and profitable work really is a possibility, you've already taken an important step toward reawakening the dreams and passions you may have had as a child. All of a sudden, complacency and "comfortable misery" become intolerable. The idea of putting your calling on the shelf becomes intolerable. Not only do we have the opportunity, we have the responsibility to spend our working hours in work that will elevate us to our highest calling and transform the world around us.

I was raised on a dairy farm in rural Ohio. My father was a farmer and the pastor of the small Mennonite church in our one-caution-light town, which gave me a unique perspective on the world. Fulfilling God's will meant honoring my father and mother, attending church at least three times a week, not swearing like my town buddies, and keeping my word. Going to ball games, swimming pools, proms, dances, and having free time was out. Fancy cars, TVs, current fashions, and other "worldly" possessions were absolutely forbidden. Work was a constant, seven-days-a-week activity. Cows needed to be milked twice a day, 365 days a year. Corn needed to be planted, hay needed to be mowed, and chicken coops needed to be cleaned.

I had little freedom to consider what kind of work I wanted to do or was called to do. Any wishes, desires, dreams, or callings were squeezed by the realities of life—work had to be done just to survive. The luxury of "enjoying" work was not discussed. Wasn't work only something we do to pass time through this earthly life until we reach our heavenly reward? Doesn't the Bible tell us that work was the resulting curse to Adam for eating from the tree of life?

> "The ground is cursed because of you. You will eat from it by means of painful labor all the days of your life. It will produce thorns and thistles for you, and you will eat the plants of the field. You will eat bread by the sweat of your brow until you return to the ground, since you were taken from it. For you are dust, and you will return to dust." (Gen. 3:17–19)

Now, I understood that "sweat of your brow" part—only physical work mattered. Those people who "worked" in town in banks, offices, and shopping malls had soft jobs and were separated from real life. Yet, out in the fields nothing could stop my mind from wandering, imagining a world I had never seen. I wanted to do more, go more, have more, and be more than anything I was seeing.

And as I continued to read Scripture on my own, I began to notice a new perspective on work. If work was a punishment for evil, why does the Bible continuously tell us to enjoy our work? Even Solomon in his most pessimistic moments told us "it is also the gift of God whenever anyone eats, drinks, and enjoys all his efforts" (Eccles. 3:13). In Colossians 3:23 we are told "whatever you do, do it enthusiastically, as something done for the Lord and not for men." And God even seems to be promising work as a reward in eternity. Surprise! The saved will "build houses and live in them; they will plant vineyards" and "will fully enjoy the work of their hands" (Isa. 65:21–22). And in Genesis 8:21 we find that after the flood, God removed that curse of the ground we read about in chapter three.

Although I was expected to continue in the family farming when I completed high school, my own desire for work that seemed a better fit for me led me to college to broaden my options. The disadvantages of a poor, legalistic upbringing were helpful in forcing me to look beyond familial expectations for a more fulfilling life. I began a path of relentless personal study alongside academic requirements for multiple degrees in psychology and religion. I wanted to see if I could blend a life committed to God with a life of meaningful work.

And what an exciting journey that has been. Along the way I worked as an adjunctive therapist in a psychiatric hospital, taught psychology at the university level, sold cars, owned a four-thousand-member health and fitness center, built an auto accessories business, painted houses, mowed lawns, counseled at a church, ran a cashew vending machine business, and sold books and informational products on the Internet.

But those experiences gave me the preparation for working with people going through their own inevitable career changes. For the last twenty years I've had the privilege of working as an author, speaker, and career coach. The foundational principles you will read in this book come from personal experience and many years of studying and coaching with those who, like myself, have found their calling.

Getting Started

48 Days to the Work You Love outlines a new process of looking at what you are going to be when you grow up. How has God uniquely gifted you in (1) *Skills and Abilities,* (2) *Personality Tendencies,* and (3) *Values, Dreams, and Passions*? From these areas you will see clear patterns from which to make career and job decisions. These patterns create a compass, providing a sense of continuity in the midst of inevitable job changes and workplace unpredictability. Looking inward provides 85 percent of the process of finding proper direction; 15 percent is the application to career choices.

Work is not a curse of God but one of the benefits of living on this earth. Finding *the work you love* is not a self-serving goal; *it is a required component of fulfilling your true calling.*

You may be asking, why *48 Days*? Well, the Bible is quite clear that God considers 40 days to be a spiritually significant time period. In fact, in the Bible, many times when God wanted to prepare people for something better, He took 40 days.

- Noah's life and the world were transformed by 40 days of rain.
- Moses was a different man after spending 40 days on Mount Sinai.
- The Israelite spies scouted the Promised Land for 40 days.
- Elijah ran more than two hundred miles in 40 days on one meal to get to a place where he could hear from God again.
- Goliath spent 40 days challenging the Israelite army while God prepared David to confront him.
- The people of Nineveh were transformed in 40 days after God's challenge to change their ways.
- Jesus was empowered for ministry by spending 40 days in the desert.
- The disciples were transformed by spending 40 days with Jesus after the Resurrection.

- There are 40 days between Ash Wednesday and Easter (not counting Sundays).

I'm giving you eight free days in the process to create your own plan. Take a break on Sundays and a couple of Saturdays. Don't knock yourself out; just stay committed to this time frame to avoid the usual procrastination.

The next 48 Days can transform your life. And yes, I do believe that 48 Days is an adequate time frame in which to assess where you are uniquely gifted, identify your strongest characteristics, get the advice of competent advisors, consider the options, choose the best path for meaningful and fulfilling work, create a plan of action, and ACT. *(See www.48Days.com/worksheets for the famous 48 Days Schedule to walk you through your own 48 Days plan.)*

This is a book where you get to tell the ending. You get to decide if the main character is a victim of circumstances, unable to rise above the oppressive forces of his or her upbringing, current family expectations, and the limitations allowed by the government and the company. But you also get to write the ending where the main character designs a life complete with work that matters, has money far beyond personal needs, builds relationships that nurture the soul, and leaves a legacy for the rest of history. While it may not be finding a white horse and riding off into the sunset, it's actually better. You get to choose.

Believing that I have been created with a purpose,
I commit the next 48 Days to a new clarity
and a plan of action for finding—or creating—work that
is meaningful, fulfilling, and profitable.

Name _____ Date _____

Chapter 1

What Is Work?

The master in the art of living makes little distinction between his work and his play, his labor and his leisure, his mind and his body, his information and his recreation, his love and his religion. He hardly knows which is which. He simply pursues his vision of excellence at whatever he does, leaving others to decide whether he is working or playing. To him he is always doing both.
— JAMES MICHENER

Is work that necessary evil that consumes the time between our brief periods of enjoyment on the weekends? Is it primarily a method of paying the bills and showing responsibility? Or a way to prove to our parents that the college degree was a reasonable investment? Or the shortest path to retirement? Or is it more?

It seems some people believe that work is a trade-off for enjoyment. That work is only done to produce a paycheck. And here's another common myth: that the more income a person makes, the higher the stress level. No, when work and passion are combined, the money flows much easier. You may be making $10 an hour and be very stressed, or you may be making $123,000 a year and love what you're doing. The issue is not how much money is being generated but rather, how much does the work "fit" you.

The *Oxford Dictionary* defines *work* as:

1. Activity involving mental or physical effort done in order to achieve a purpose or result,
2. Mental or physical activity as a means of earning income; employment,
3. Employment, as in some form of industry, especially as a means of earning one's livelihood, or
4. The place where one works.[1]

We seem to contrast this definition of work with play. Surely we can escape work to spend time in play.

The same dictionary defines *play* as:

1. Engage in (a game or activity) for enjoyment,
2. Amuse oneself by engaging in imaginative pretense, or
3. Be part of a team, especially in a specified position, in a game.

To work is to carry out the duties of a job; to play is to do something enjoyable. But what if you found something you truly enjoyed that also supplied your needed income? Would work and play actually become one and the same? Is it unreasonable to expect our work to be an enjoyable activity? Is that really such an impossible idea? What would happen to your plans for "retirement" if you were doing work that was meaningful and profitable now? Isn't our idea of retirement to be able to quit this stinking job and be able to do something enjoyable every day? What a novel idea.

People often ask me if I'm living the life I'm talking about. And I tell them to come spend a couple of days with me to then decide for themselves. You can see the schedule of events here (www.48Days.com/liveevents). On the back-side of our property we have an old barn that we've redeemed and converted into my office, an event center, and guest quarters. My commute in the morning is free of traffic lights, horns, bad roads, and angry people fighting to get to their place of work. Outside my office window I see a waterfall and bird feeders that attract colorful birds and wild turkeys all year long. I also see the platform for a zip-line we put up a few years ago that runs 350 feet from my office down over the nature trail, past my little red barn and right to the back door of our house. My grandchildren are free to come and play at any time.

Finding or creating the work environment that fits you is a very individualized process. Depending on your personality you could easily be bored with my workspace. I think, dream, imagine, and write as my work. If you are a social, gregarious person, my work environment would likely make you feel lonely and isolated. That's the beauty of knowing how we can shape our choices to fit what we know about ourselves. You get to choose what blends your talents, personality, and passions.

What if we check out a couple other words that are thrown in with work and play? *Leisure* is "time when you are not working: time when you can do whatever you want to do."[2] The word comes from a term in an old French dialect—*leissor,* which means "permission," or literally "to be allowed."

Let's look at how our common phrases confirm that "work" is something we have to do, while "play" is something we get to do. "Thank God it's Friday" reinforces the idea that at last we can escape the evil of work and do something we truly enjoy. "Oh no, it's Monday" clearly reinforces the message from the Mamas and the Papas' 1966 song that we "can't trust that day." Our anticipation of retirement implies that finally we can quit this thing called work and spend our time doing only what we enjoy.

But that raises the question: What would you call your daily activity if you actually enjoyed it? Would it cease to be "work"?

If the only goal of our working is to accumulate enough money to quit working, then it confirms the picture that work is just a bitter pill to be endured until the moment you can escape it. But as you move into work of your choosing and design, work that integrates your strongest talents and gifts, you will experience a joy not commonly connected with "work." And you'll find that your desire to quit and move into the blank state of retirement will diminish significantly.

The definition of *retire* is . . .

1. to stop a job or career because you have reached the age when you do not need or want to work anymore
2. to withdraw from action or danger
3. to leave a place, position, or way of life and go to a place of less activity, or
4. to withdraw from usual use or service.[3]

Isn't that what is implied when people talk about retirement? *When can I stop this stupid job and start doing what I really enjoy?* Do you really want to stop engaging in daily activities? Or withdraw from service? Instead, why not expect enjoyment in your daily work?

The fruits of a fulfilling life—happiness, confidence, enthusiasm, purpose, and money—are mainly by-products of doing something we enjoy, with excellence, rather than things we can seek directly.

In his popular book *The Millionaire Mind,* Thomas J. Stanley, Ph.D., looks at the characteristics of America's wealthiest people, attempting to identify their distinguishing traits. Is it their IQ, GPA, college major, family's opportunity, or business selection? Surprisingly, none of these topics seems to predict their extraordinary success. The one characteristic the millionaires did have in common is *they were all doing something they loved.* Dr. Stanley concludes, "If you love, absolutely love what you are doing, chances are excellent that you will succeed."[4]

Our early ideas of work tend to view it as something less than desirable and enjoyable. Tom, a sharp twenty-seven-year-old, came to my office wanting confirmation that he was on the right track. He had recently graduated from college (having finished the seven-year plan) and had taken a sales position with an office-equipment company. Each morning he put on his suit and made his calls. The company loved him, but he was bored beyond belief. I asked him why he had taken this route, and his reply relayed a common perception. Tom said that he had a great time in college—traveling, snowboarding, attending ball games, and spending time with his friends. After graduation, he felt it was time to "grow up" and become part of the "real world." He assumed that meant getting a job he hated to prove his responsibility.

I laughed and asked who had sold him that bill of goods. We looked carefully at his skills, personality traits, values, dreams, and passions. Today, Tom is co-owner of a snowboard shop in Breckenridge, Colorado. On a moonlit night you might catch him coming down a hill, testing one of his new designs.

 Abused Wife Syndrome

No, this excerpt is not really about abused wives, but I had a client use that term recently in describing his repeated return to the unfulfilling work of his professional training. In his mind, there was a strikingly similar pattern. He would break away from the work he despised for something more rewarding, experience a challenge or setback, and return to the dreaded work, knowing it was where he could make the most predictable income.

Do you do your work only because of its paycheck? Do you long to leave for something more enjoyable? Have you tried another path only to return to what is more familiar? Many people often get trapped in these patterns of returning to negative, abusive situations. The emotions and self-esteem issues there may be complicated and confusing. However, the stakes are dramatically lessened with a job.

A job should not define who or what you are. You should be able to leave today and it not change the overall purpose or direction of your life. Your calling is a much larger concept than what you do daily to create income. Work opportunities can come and go—the direction of your life should remain constant.

Why Do We Work?

In asking this question, I typically get the following responses:

- to pay the bills
- for food, clothing, and shelter
- because of others' expectations
- to combat boredom
- for self-worth
- for social stimulation
- because it's a place to go

I encounter a lot of people who leave their traditional jobs because they want to do something more significant. One woman, who has just resigned from her $74,000-per-year job, said she wanted to do something "noble." Many are saying they want to make a difference, to make the world a better place, and to do something with *spiritual* significance.

Now there's another word worth checking out—*spiritual,* meaning . . .

1. of or relating to a person's spirit
2. concerned with religious values[5]

You mean normal work does not connect our mind, spirit, and temperament? Perhaps we can create a definition of *work* that includes more than just completing duties for a paycheck. What if we were able to create a model for work that included work, play, leisure, and spiritual components?

Would it be unreasonable to expect to find fulfilling, enjoyable, spiritually significant, income-producing work?

In his book *Prayer,* Richard Foster says, "The work of our hands and of our minds is acted out prayer, a love offering to the living God."[6] Kahlil Gibran adds, "Work is love made visible."[7] Is that how you feel about your work—that it's a prayer offering to God? That it is a direct expression of how you love others? Or are you thinking that perhaps God looks the other way when you go to work?

How is it possible for our work to be a form of prayer? This may seem challenging as long as we think of prayer as something we do only on our knees with folded hands and closed eyes. But if we recognize prayer as a time of being present with God, then it follows that our work can be a form of engaging our hearts and spirits in a way that places us in His presence. Anything less would be a questionable use of our time, talent, and resources.

We live in a time that gives us the luxury of seeing the benefits of work that go beyond just providing a paycheck. Money is ultimately never enough compensation for investing one's time and energy. There must be a sense of purpose, meaning, and accomplishment. Remember psychologist Abraham Maslow's famous hierarchy of needs:

1. First, I need *food, water, air, rest,* etc. (Basic physiological needs)
2. Second, I need *safety* and *security.* (Do I have stability and structure?)
3. I need to *belong* and feel *loved.* (Does anybody like me?)
4. Next comes *self-esteem.* (Do I feel competent and appreciated?)
5. Lastly, I need *self-actualization.* (Am I doing what I'm suited for/talented at?)[8]

Most of us aren't worried about finding food tonight, but we are concerned about if we are spending our time doing something meaningful. Having a job that provides nothing more than safety and security is not very fulfilling.

 Crushed Spirit

I recently saw a sixty-one-year-old gentleman who lost his job nine months ago. When a long period of unemployment has passed, I always suspect more life issues to be lurking in the sidelines. Sure enough, his wife left him four months ago, his daughter ("the joy of my life") got married and moved away five months ago, his investments are now worth less than half of what they were three years ago, his place of employment for thirty-six years let him go with a small severance package, he's unconnected at his church, and feels "rejected on all sides." He made the last mortgage payment three weeks ago on his dream house that now must be sold to settle the divorce before he moves into an apartment in town.

Where do we go from there? Proverbs 18:14 tells us "a man's spirit can endure sickness, but who can survive a broken spirit?" Or in the Living Bible "what hope is left?"

Each area of our lives requires us to make deposits of success. Tiny withdrawals with no deposits will lead to physical, spiritual, and emotional bankruptcy in relationships, jobs, and finances. In times of crisis the area of most pain gets the most attention, but by making extra deposits in other areas, we can bounce back to success in our most depleted accounts.

My advice: Set aside time for vigorous physical exercise. Walk three miles four or five times a week—the feeling will help release tension and stimulate creativity. Seek out an inspiring mentor. Much of the success of Alcoholics Anonymous has been from attendees having another person to call in the lowest times. Read inspirational material at least two hours daily. Volunteer for a worthy cause—helping someone else in need is a great way to ease the inward pain. Get a job even if it's not your dream job or a great career move. Deliver pizzas or work in the garden department at Home Depot to get moving in a positive direction while you continue to build for long-term success.

Unfortunately, some losses are irretrievable and some pain is debilitating. If you recognize too many withdrawals in your life, take drastic measures to stop the hemorrhaging today!

How Do We Choose Work?

The opportunities in today's work environment are endless. While in previous generations children adopted the careers handed down by their parents, today's youth have little or no guidance to direct them onto a work path. They enter the workplace with little work experience and little knowledge of varied careers, leading to poorly made life-directing decisions. Often, a career decision is made with less thought and planning than is put into deciding where to go for spring break. When I asked a young college graduate how he chose criminal justice as his major, he said, "On the first day of college they sent all of us freshmen into a big room. Then they announced, 'If you are going into accounting, follow this lady down the hall. Advertising majors, go this way.' I looked down the list [of majors], closed my eyes, and hit the page with my finger. Criminal justice became my chosen field."

Don't laugh. It's a frequently used process. Who knows how to choose the right major? Many business administration majors discovered during their junior year that the quickest way to graduation was by declaring that major. I'm now starting to see graduates with degrees in university studies. Was it just too challenging to decide on any focus? Next we'll have a degree in "showing up." That's why ten years after graduation, 80 percent of college graduates are working in something totally unrelated to their college major. And that's okay. College is a broadening experience that rarely forces anyone into a narrow tunnel of no escape. You can change course several times in a lifetime without feeling like you're derailed or starting over, if you have a sense of calling to act as a constant compass. More on that in chapter 3.

 "The Shallow Waters of Avarice"

One question on my coaching request form is "Briefly describe your current work situation." Here is a response from a thirty-three-year-old guy:

"Antithetical to my personal and professional expectations. Unfulfilling on multiple levels: Lack of meaning and purpose; a myopic pursuit of the almighty dollar; a parasitic and never-ending voyage into the shallow waters of avarice."

Wow. What a powerful and eloquent statement of being off track and realizing that money is never enough compensation for investing one's time and energy.

He continued: "Because of the necessity and immediacy of my situation . . . I took the path of least resistance, which has led me down a perilous pike of disappointment and despair. As a direct result of our financial obligations, I absolved myself of the freedom to pursue my dreams for the oppressive restraints of debt." Feeling trapped by the realities of life, he felt blocked from any attempts at following his true passions.

Fortunately, new possibilities are possible. We mapped out a process for getting an additional degree and an immediate plan for expression of his unique writing skills. He can hike, run a marathon, study fossils with his kids, and get involved in a book club. Life does not have to be put on hold. There are always ways to make deposits of success in areas deemed important. Few obstacles exist beyond those in our minds if we are creative in looking for solutions. And remember to enjoy the journey, starting with today. Success is not a future event—it is the *progressive realization of worthwhile goals*. Thus, either you are successful today or you are not.

Look for opportunities to rise above the "shallow waters of avarice" today.

———————

Generational expectations still do play a large role in many career decisions. Historically each generation has been expected to be more educated and wealthier than the preceding one. Many in preceding generations had the finest degrees, invested in rapidly growing companies, and banked millions. Now what are their offspring supposed to do to top that? Or here's a situation: What if the son of a cardiologist is really gifted as a carpenter? Can we encourage that young man to be excellent as a carpenter, or will he be railroaded into a "professional" career?

Several years ago I saw a young surgeon who had gone to Harvard Medical School, as had his father and grandfather. He had the finest cars and opportunities along the way. And yet something was amiss. By the time he came to see me, he was shooting heroin into the heels of his feet (the heels being the only parts of his body where he had not abused the veins). He had been admitted to a psychiatric hospital in an attempt to save his life. While working with me, he expressed his childhood dream of driving a truck.

Today he works as an emergency room physician on the weekends and is still able to make a significant income. During the week he drives a snack delivery truck. He has moved out to the country and is getting his life in order.

Proverbs 22:6 says, "Teach a youth about the way he should go; even when he is old he will not depart from it." That verse has been distorted to justify cramming spiritual principles onto impressionable children to make certain their theology matches that of their parents. And to force a child to move up academically and socioeconomically from the parents. A truer reading of the original text might be: "Train up a child in the way that he is bent . . ." The challenge of parenting is to discover how God has uniquely gifted this child and how the parent can help the child excel in that area. Thus there will be times when the son of a surgeon will be most gifted as a truck driver or carpenter or musician or missionary. Well-intentioned parents, teachers, pastors, and others in positions of influence can easily misdirect an impressionable child if external opportunities are the only criteria for career selection. The power of confidence in career choice comes from looking inward for the alignment of personal characteristics, not from looking outward to where "opportunities" lie.

Here are some more misdirected influences in choosing a career:

- What will be in the most demand? With entire industries becoming obsolete in four to five years, how can we accurately predict the jobs of the future?
- What are the most "godly," "humanitarian," or "socially or environmentally responsible" careers? While honorable, using these as external criteria can misdirect a person from doing what is a proper "fit."
- What is the most secure? *Security* is a slippery concept in today's work environment. Little security is found in any company or job. The only security is in understanding yourself—that will provide a compass for navigating the inevitable changes.
- How can I achieve position, status, and power? This is likely to be an elusive path, leading to rapid burnout.
- Where can I get the greatest income? (Similar to the previous bullet point.) If you look first at the money, it will likely stay just outside your grasp.
- What is advertised in online job bulletins? Probably the worst of all influences, it has nothing to do with your uniqueness or a proper alignment of your calling.

None of these will help you build a *life plan*. Even as we focus on the work aspect of our lives, be very aware that getting a job is only one tool for creating a meaningful life.

Better questions to ask regarding a career or job choice would be:

- What was I born to do?
- What would be my greatest contribution to others?
- What do I really love to do (and when I'm doing it, time just flies by)?
- What are the recurring themes that I find myself drawn to?
- How do I want to be remembered?

When we are not true to ourselves, to our unique God-given characteristics, we lose the power of authenticity, creativity, imagination, and innovation. Our life becomes performance-based, setting the stage for compromise in all other areas of our lives.

Countdown to Work I Love

1. Who gave you your first job? What kind of job was it? How much money did you make?

2. From looking at your work life so far, what has been of the greatest value or worth?

3. If your job changes, does your *calling* change?

4. Do you think your current job will exist five years from now?

5. What would be the key characteristics of an ideal job or career?

6. When you daydream, what do you see yourself doing?

7. What have been the happiest, most fulfilling moments in your life?

8. If nothing changed in your life in the next five years, would that be okay?

Chapter 2

Who Would Hire Me?

---

*"You have brains in your head. You have feet in your shoes.
You can steer yourself any direction you choose. You're on
your own. And you know what you know. And YOU are the
one who'll decide where to go . . ."*
—Dr. Seuss, *Oh, the Places You'll Go!*

How do you make yourself a top candidate in today's workplace?

Don't the smartest people with the best degrees always get ahead? Is it luck that allows someone to get hired? Why do some folks get multiple job offers when others are convinced the economy is bad and no one is hiring?

A young gentleman in the banking industry invited me to lunch. I met John about ten years earlier when he was just a teller and hadn't seen him since then. The day of our lunch he pulled up to the restaurant in a gorgeous new Infinity, had on a stunning suit, and told me about his new position as the community director of a very powerful bank. I knew little about what had transpired for him in those last ten years—but I did know he was in an industry that had been struggling with well-publicized downsizings and terminations.

However, it was easy to observe why this guy has excelled. Every encounter I observed was courteous and affirming for the other person. From the greeter, to the servers, to the random people walking by, each one received a great smile and a sincere "thank you" for their contribution, no matter how small or insignificant. I didn't have to ask about additional degrees, certifications, or inside favors to understand why his career has soared. He doesn't have to hope the economy is good in order to keep his job. In fact, he told me of the constant offers he was receiving from competitors who had seen his success. And he was making more money than he ever dreamed of a few years before.

He had guaranteed his position, not through manipulation or asserting his rights or having a contract, but by being a person everyone wants on their team.

That sounds strangely familiar—like it's right out of a book written in 1936, right after the Great Depression.

Six Ways to Make People Like You:

1. Become genuinely interested in other people.
2. Smile.
3. Remember that a person's name is to that person the sweetest and most important sound in any language.
4. Be a good listener. Encourage others to talk about themselves.
5. Talk in terms of the other person's interests.
6. Make the other person feel important—and do it sincerely.[1]

I have no idea if John has a college degree. But I know how his value would rank against most MBA graduates. Those six principles will do more to open doors of opportunity than being in the right place at the right time, luck, degrees, or stellar GPA. And fortunately, you don't have to wait, take out a student loan, or get a special break from Uncle Harry to start using them to your advantage.

Have you guaranteed your job security?

I talk to too many people today who are looking for "safety" and "security." With those as your goals you are almost certain to miss the best opportunities. Those terms imply old and pre-dictable—certainly not new, innovative, full of potential with open-ended income possibilities. Beware of safe and secure—they will trap you in the common, mediocre life. I talked to a young man who, with his wife and new baby, were moving back into his grandparents' house. The grandparents had made it clear that they wanted to be in charge of raising that little girl—even expressing it as "we want another chance to raise a child right." Past experi-ence tells us that this relationship would be destructive—but the rent was free. I reminded the young father that there's always free cheese in a mousetrap.

Now Will the Government Guarantee Me a Job?

In a 2012 Presidential debate, one of the questions from the audience came from a twenty-one-year-old college student named Jeremy, who asked both candidates: "What can you say to reassure me, but more importantly my parents, that I will be able to suf-ficiently support myself after I graduate?"

Unfortunately, both candidates gave political answers to this young man, playing into the idea that this student's success is somehow dependent on government policies or who is in the White House. One candidate promised he would continue the student loan policies—which have led to insurmountable debt for gradu-ates and a 25 percent spike in tuition. He said he would make it easier to go to college—a system that is turning out thousands of graduates who have few marketable skills. He even mentioned that half of recent graduates were unemployed or severely underem-ployed. Adding more to this number is not reassuring—it should be terrifying.

The other candidate promised Jeremy that he would increase manufacturing and factory jobs. However, as a life coach I don't encounter many college graduates who identify working in a fac-tory as their dream destination. Most want to avoid the life of their parents and follow paths that embrace their passions. They want to be part of a worthy cause and do something to change the world.

> *"Playing it safe is like body surfing in two feet of water. You may not drown, but you're also not in deep enough to catch any but the most meager of waves. The most dangerous strategy is to play it safe. In its place, Break-It Thinkers take risks and break rules and challenge convention, making change an ally."* —Robert Kriegel[2]

Yes, politicians get elected by telling us what they are going to "give" us, but Jeremy needs to be reminded that "circumstances" will never assure him any kind of success. The economy can be robust and unemployment at zero and it will have little to do with his success. This is very much an inner game—not determined by external factors.

The real question is—Jeremy, why would someone want to hire you? What have you done to bring value to the table for my company? What are your three strongest personal characteristics? What projects have you headed up in the last two years? What makes you remarkable?

Here's what I would tell Jeremy:

1. Understand the need for *wisdom* as an addition to knowledge and information. You may have knowledge and degrees, but know that wisdom is the meaningful application of that knowledge.
2. Understand the changing models of work—thousands are finding legitimate work models and extraordinary income as consultants, contingency workers, independent contractors, freelancers, and entrepreneurs. The old days of thinking the 8-to-5 job, with two weeks' vacation and medical benefits, is the only viable option are over.
3. Make your life international—meet new friends. Seek to understand those with different cultural experiences, different customs, and different faiths.

4. Understand the power of relationships—the African concept of Ubuntu, where "they" become "we." We cannot be fully human alone. Look for opportunities to connect and help others succeed.

5. Serve those around you—don't wait until you graduate. If you want more money just figure out how to serve more people.

6. Have a pleasing personality—be generous with your resources, keep your word, smile easily, listen well, and honor the uniqueness of each person you meet.

7. Know your gifts and talents—what makes you remarkable. Don't rely on degrees alone to open doors of opportunity.

Yes, Jeremy, follow these seven steps and I can reassure you and your parents—with confidence—that you will be well able to sufficiently support yourself after you graduate. Follow those seven steps and you can be assured you will be able to follow your passion, create extraordinary income, and make the world a better place.

 Will an MBA Open All the Doors?

A reader asked: "Dan, I am thirty-two years old and I have just started an MBA program at Auburn University because I have spent the past five years in a very technical/engineering position at the bottom of the corporate ladder. I picked the MBA route because with each company I have evaluated a lot of the upper management had their MBAs. Since my desire has always been to be a market leader, I just assumed that an MBA would be a requirement. What really separates a résumé/person from a CEO position in a Fortune 500 company?" Hopeful, Tina

Tina, I commend you on moving forward and not being content with the status quo. You are right to question what it is that separates a "résumé person" from a CEO. And it's never just a matter of having the right degrees. Actually, it's less that now than ever before. Here at 48 Days LLC we have engaged a social media director, product fulfillment manager, webmaster, graphic designers, blog coach, podcast consultant, speech coach, marketing director, and several other positions. In not one case did I ask for a résumé or even inquire about degrees or certifications.

More likely I am going to look for:

1. Notes of recommendation from three people I know and respect.
2. A past project I can review.
3. Media buzz about what that person has already done.
4. Leadership of a group on a social networking site.
5. A regular blog that is compelling and engaging.
6. A high EQ (Emotional Quotient) vs a high IQ.

You may say, "Well, I don't have any of those things." Then that begs the question: Why would someone see you as an outstanding candidate?

Unfortunately, the MBA has become a very common and generic degree. No one knows what it really means other than you have shown the discipline to stick with a program for a couple of years. It is also the degree most often added to a résumé dishonestly. Seldom are degrees checked and there are thousands of people who have added MBA to their résumé, hoping for a little extra edge.

I would encourage you to be building your reputation in ways like those noted above that will get attention and open doors all around you. The days of a great résumé being enough are over. You have to be remarkable in other ways.

———

Your Diploma Has Expired

Here's an interesting thought. We recognize that many things have a "shelf life"—the length of time that foods, beverages, medicine, and other items are given before they are considered unsuitable for sale, use, or consumption. Upon the "expiration date" those items are seen to be of little use, or even dangerous.

We know that much of what a college freshman learns will be obsolete before they graduate. So why would we, in a rapidly changing workplace, think the value of a diploma will last forever?

The expiration date of pharmaceuticals specifies the date the manufacturer guarantees the full potency and safety of a drug. Why don't universities specify the length of time a degree will be fully applicable and useful?

When I graduated from The Ohio State University, I was required to take a computer course to be eligible for a BA degree. I took FORTRAN. The best I can remember it was developed in 1958 as an early version of programming. Today it's right up there with the rotary phone in terms of usefulness. My diploma should have estimated the value of that to expire in perhaps ten years.

Imagine you have a degree in biology. Will the knowledge we have now be current ten years from now? Of course not. Your diploma has a built-in expiration date—we just don't like to be up front about that. Universities don't want to stamp on your degree— "Good for the next fifteen years." Consequently, we pretend to do great work with the knowledge we gathered twenty or thirty years ago. And as a result, we stifle innovation and opportunity.

I know, there's the pressure in having a degree to get a return on your investment to justify the time and expense invested. But new opportunities appear every day. The workplace does not stay the same. You do not stay the same. You may discover and develop skills that would lend themselves to a completely unrelated career path.

People feel stuck because of "too much" education and because of "not enough" education. I have an attorney friend who is "too educated to move on" to something that would blend the best of his skills, talents, and passions. And of course I have encountered many people who are convinced they are not trained enough to be candidates for what their hearts are calling them to.

We need to broaden our understanding of what constitutes "education."

The World Doesn't Pay You for What You Know, But For . . .

Okay, I'll go ahead and finish the sentence:

The world doesn't pay you for what you know, but for what you do. I guess we would all acknowledge the truth of that, and yet I am amazed at the number of people I run into who are bogged down in analyzing, learning, planning, and organizing when what they really need to do is take action. I think more than anything else that's what separates winners from losers—the winners take action.

I once saw Jack Canfield demonstrate this in a seminar. He held up a $100 bill and asked, "Who wants this $100 bill?" People all over the room said, "I do" or "Please pick me." And Jack just stood there waving that $100 bill and kept asking, "Who wants this $100 bill?" Finally, someone jumped out of her seat, ran to the front, and grabbed it out of his hand. He then asked, "What did she do that no one else did?" Right, she took action.

If you were in that room, you may share in the reasons given by those still in their seats:

- "I didn't want to look like I needed it that badly."
- "I wasn't sure if you would really give it to me."
- "I thought someone else would get there first."
- "I figured there must be a trick somewhere—you wouldn't really give it away."
- "I didn't want to look greedy."
- "I was waiting for further instructions."

And then Jack gently pointed out that the things we say to ourselves are probably the same things we are saying that are stopping us in other areas of our lives. If you are cautious here, you are probably cautious everywhere. If you hold back for fear of looking foolish, you probably hold back for fear of looking foolish in most situations. If you needed more instructions here, you probably find yourself needing more instructions before moving ahead. If you assume it's already been done or someone else will surely beat you to it, you may be missing more unique opportunities.

Henry Ford said, "You can't build a reputation on what you are going to do."[3]

Any success I've had has come as a result of just doing something—most of the time before I had done a lot of research or planning. The first version of *48 Days to the Work You Love* had an ugly blue cover printed at Kinkos, held together with a spiral binding. Then we added a free-standing cassette recording that I did at a friend's house. No editing, no correcting, no music intros. We just put a rough version together and people started buying. If I had waited until I knew how to do everything right, I probably would have missed the first $1 million in sales.

What do you need to start DOING?

The Educated Unemployed

I'll bet you can name ten people with fancy college degrees who are struggling to find work right now. Or they just took the difficulty of finding work as a reason to go back and get another degree—confident that with another piece of paper someone will "give" them a job.

Do you know research indicates our universities are graduating exactly ten times more psychology majors each year than there are jobs for psychology majors? But are college guidance counselors telling these bright-eyed kids, "There will be a job for only one in every ten of you. The rest of you will have to figure out some other way to repay your student loans and make a living." Of course not. We encourage even more to get that degree in psychology, political science, graphic design, or for the chronically indecisive—"university studies."

Of course, if you are unsure about a clear focus, you can take classes (yes, these are all real class offerings) in *The Art of Walking, Maple Syrup, Tightwaddery, The American Vacation, Finding Dates Worth Keeping,* or *The Amazing World of Bubbles.*

Is it any wonder we have growing numbers of "Educated Unemployed" in our ranks? Recently, an HR professional told me she has interviewed more than eleven hundred people in the last twelve months. And in her words, many of them were "over-educated" and felt entitled to a high level position without having to prove their value in advance.

Oh yes, I have a BA in Psychology and an MA in Clinical Psychology. Very enjoyable studies and I learned a lot about myself. And then I figured out how to make a living.

What in your training or experience makes you "employable"? What value do you bring to the table—whether or not you have a degree?

"Overqualified"

I don't want to hurt your feelings so I'll just say you're "overqualified."

I've never turned down an applicant because I felt he or she was overqualified, and frankly, I don't think anyone does.

I was approached by a young man recently after a presentation. His question was—*"What do you do when you're overqualified for any job available?"* He proceeded to tell me he had a Master's degree in Public Health and had been told in multiple interviews he was "overqualified."

Now think about the reality here—in what setting would being "overqualified" eliminate you from consideration? If my mechanic gets an additional certification will I tell him, "I don't want you working on my car anymore—I'm afraid you're too smart"? If you show up for a simple physical exam and find out the doctor is a cardiologist, will you back off because he's overqualified? If you are choosing a massage therapist and discover that one contender has a PhD in anatomy, will you eliminate that person? If you need a receptionist with a great personality, would you reject the candidate you liked the most if you discovered at the last minute that she had a Masters in English Literature? Would you send a carpenter away because he had too much experience?

As in any of these situations the only justification for telling a person they are "overqualified" is likely found in this list:

- We think you're overselling your abilities.
- We don't think you'd be a team player here.
- We don't like you.
- We don't trust you.
- You want too much money.
- We think you're too arrogant and condescending.
- We suspect you'll leave as soon as you find something better.

Please hear my gentle counsel—being told you are "too experienced" or "overqualified" is simply a politically correct way of telling you they aren't convinced they want you on their team. This statement is a *disguise*—and a safe way to make it sound like the person is complimenting you. But it doesn't realistically have anything to do with your qualifications, knowledge, or talent. It's a meaningless term that protects the company from being candid about the real reason they don't see you as a good choice. Forget about your degrees—work on interview skills that make people like you, trust you, and want to be around you.

To help maintain our property we hired a young man as our "yard beauty manager." We were only looking for someone to maintain our flowerbeds and keep them free of weeds. I had thirty-five to forty people apply who could pull weeds and just wanted a job. This young man has a degree in horticulture, is licensed and bonded in the state of Tennessee, ignored my hourly pay offer, and gave me a four-page proposal for year-round care. Did I reject him because he was clearly more "overqualified" than any other candidate? No, I loved his in-depth knowledge. But the thing that really tipped the scale was that both Joanne and I just liked him as a person. We felt comfortable with him, appreciated his respect and his focus on making our property beautiful rather than on how soon he could get paid.

Incidentally, the young man I referred to earlier who was convinced he was "overqualified" was very defensive, convinced it was purely his brilliance, qualifications, and superior ability that made people feel inferior around him and he was helpless to change that reality. I rest my case.

Has anyone ever suggested you were "overqualified"? What was the message you felt in your gut?

If you're hearing this phrase a lot in your interviews, look for the real reason you're not getting opportunities. I am confident it falls in line with one of the bullet points above. There's no such thing as "overqualified."

 ## The Challenge of Change

"Is there still time for me to make my life count?" Recently I met a twenty-seven-year-old who asked me this very question. "Please tell me," he continued, "that just because I started as an attorney doesn't mean my life will be filed away . . . Encourage me to find a motivating desire once more. I think I've lost it."

Is it too late for this misdirected twenty-seven-year-old? When do we reach the point of no return and have to settle for the life we have chosen or had chosen for us?

People are increasingly saying, "I still don't know what I want to do when I grow up." And this is coming not only from the twenty-year-olds but from those in their forties and fifties as well. People often say this with embarrassment, but the search for clear meaning should be a continued one for each of us. It's healthy at any point to draw that line in the sand and ask, "Who am I?" and "Why am I here?" If you are still living out your life based on decisions made when you were eighteen, you may have reason to be concerned. Things have changed. You have changed.

Why would someone stay in a position they clearly dislike? Is it being responsible to continue day after day in work that does not embrace our strongest talents and passions? Is it a commitment to responsibility or fear that keeps us in a situation like that? I think it's fear. When I offer a seminar on changing jobs or starting businesses, the one question that comes up more than any other is, "How do I get over my fear of moving in any new direction?" And then people ask, "What if I attempt something new and fail? How could I possibly start over?"

"Successful Failure"

"Dan, I would like to hear more of your thoughts on failure. Since most of us are probably going to fail several times, what does a 'successful failure' look like? How much should we risk in pursuit of our dreams? As you often say, we must not be paralyzed by our fear of failure but I doubt you would suggest that we risk our marriages, health, homes, etc., while seeking to reach our goals. What do you think is the right balance in this area?" Thanks, Evan

Great question, Evan. And I believe there really are "successful failures" in life. That is not an oxymoron. Napoleon Hill once said: "Failure seems to be nature's plan for preparing us for great responsibilities."[4]

So part of the issue is—do you want to do something great—in any area? If you are content with mediocrity in your life, then you will try to protect yourself from any failure. Just recognize the trade-off.

But here's an important distinction: It's not just what you do in a job or your business that will identify you as a success or a failure.

Not having "date nights" or saying, "I love you" daily will put your marriage at risk of failure.

Spending sixty-five hours a week at your job will put your emotional well-being at risk of failure.

Eating Twinkies and Big Macs and not exercising will put your health at risk of failure.

Financing a car or paying more than the equivalent of one month's income in cash will put your financial health at risk of failure.

Spending less than an hour a day on spiritual and personal development sets you up for the risk of failure.

Expecting a company to continue giving you a paycheck puts you at risk of failure.

These are ways people set themselves up for "failure" totally aside from whether they pursue a suitable work option. The counterpart to this is, if you are successful in all the areas mentioned above, then "failure" in a job or business venture is not crippling. It is simply one area in which to readjust and start again. I've heard that Richard Branson will not invest in any company unless the person in charge has failed at least twice. I'm convinced that had I not had a major failure in business a few years ago—leaving me with a $430,000 loss—that I would have continued with an unrealistic view of my golden touch. I think I needed that experience to open my eyes—not to make me cynical, but to help me create a more solid business structure going forward.

I'm also totally convinced that someone who commits suicide upon losing a job or business had neglected excellence and success in the more important areas of life. Having rich deposits in relationships, spiritual well-being, health and social connections act as a buffer in carrying you through any temporary business failure. Whether you have a job, volunteer your time, or start the next Microsoft—none of these alone will determine the success of your life.

So here's what I recommend for risking in the work areas of our lives:

- Take responsibility for where you are—whether good or bad.
- Continue making deposits of success in the physical, spiritual, personal development, and relationship areas of your life.
- Pursue work that engages your passions as well as your abilities.

- Weigh the financial requirements very carefully. Personally, I have seven different areas of revenue generation in my small business. That way if one "fails" it's not devastating.
- Recognize that a temporary financial loss does not need to be the end of your business venture. It's probably just a wake-up call, helping you to readjust for bigger successes in the future. Make the adjustment and know that you are now closer to ultimate success.

So, Evan, recognize that many people "risk failure in their marriages, health, homes, etc.," while desperately trying to hang on to a "real job." Identifying your passion, creating a careful plan of action, and moving into a new work venture may be the very thing to reduce risk and increase your opportunity for true success. Thanks for asking.

Try and Fail? Or Not Try at All?

Every year or so I like to pull out the movie *Lions for Lambs*. In this movie a brilliant but apathetic student asks his professor (played by Robert Redford), "Is there any difference in trying but failing, and simply failing to try—if you end up in the same place anyway?" He was attempting to justify taking the safe route, never really taking a stand or trying anything big.

What do you think? Do you cringe at trying something big because of the possibility of failure? What if you tried for the promotion but failed to get it, started a business but lost your investment, or tried a MLM system but got nothing other than a garage full of vitamins—are you somehow better off? Would your life have been better if you had avoided the hassle and the disappointment altogether?

Yes, I hear from people every day that tried and failed. One gentleman lost $11 million in a gas and oil business. Another lost $3.2 million inherited from his grandmother in a failed retail clothing business. A close friend lost $24 million in a failed real estate development. Research shows that if you are under thirty years old, there is a 90 percent chance you will be fired sometime in the next twenty years. Bernie Marcus was fired from a job as manager of the Handy Dan Improvement Center, then went on to start Home Depot. A few years ago I experienced a horrible "failure" in business—having to borrow a car to drive to start generating income again. Should I have avoided the pain and anguish by taking a safer route, or was that experience the necessary catalyst for learning the principles that launched the success I enjoy today? *My theory is that you will be a brighter, better person for trying something big—even if you "fail."*

I can't find the quotation I once heard so I'll improvise, but essentially it's this:

"If failure is not a possibility then winning is not so sweet." Think about it: when you play a football game, the possibility of losing is what makes winning so stinking rewarding. Isn't that how it is with just about everything? I hear from people every day who have nice big guaranteed salaries—and they're bored out of their minds. It's the people who strike out into uncharted waters who get the thrill of victory.

I'm totally confident of this: If you're not trying something right now where you have a strong possibility of failure, you're life is boring. I want to constantly be trying new things where I have a 50/50 chance of succeeding. All the major things I'm doing this year had the potential to not work—and the jury is still out on some.

What has your life experience taught you about trying big things? Have you learned to keep a low profile to avoid failure? Or have you found that "failure" leads to bigger successes?

Anytime There Is Change, There Are Seeds of Opportunity

Do you see change as a provider of new opportunities or as a threat to expected security? What is "security"? Is it a guaranteed future? A company that provides medical benefits, vacation time, and a retirement plan? Not anymore. Security today is not likely to come from a job, a company, or the government. General Douglas MacArthur said, "Security lies in our ability to produce."[5]

Contrast MacArthur's definition with George's. George has been with the same company for twenty-three years but hates his job. He has missed much of his children's lives, works on his wife's day off, and his health is deteriorating. But he can't imagine leaving the "security" of his job.

Now let me tell you how they catch monkeys in Africa. The natives take a coconut and at one end cut a hole just large enough for a monkey's hand to enter. The other end of the coconut is attached to a long rope. They then carve out the inside of the coconut and put a few peanuts inside. They place the coconut in a clearing and hide in the trees with the end of the rope. The monkeys come around, smell the peanuts, and reach inside to grab a fistful. But now, with a fistful, their hand is too large to retract through the small hole. Then the natives yank on the cord and haul that silly monkey to captivity because the monkey will not let go of those few lousy peanuts he thought he wanted. Ouch! Does that sound like a company policy?

Your only "security" is knowing what you do well. Knowing your *areas of competence* will give you freedom amid corporate politics and unexpected layoffs. Wayne Gretzky was once asked why he was such a great hockey player. He responded with an eloquent morsel of wisdom: "I simply went to where the puck *was going to be*." An average player would go where the puck was or is.

Change is inevitable, but there are upsides of change. Forest fires clean out the undergrowth and thus protect the tallest trees from danger. Many environmentalists have been obsessed with preventing any controlled fires to eliminate undergrowth, and consequently, we have seen major forest fires in the last few years. All that undergrowth provides a perfect setting for a major uncontrollable disaster when the inevitable fire does come. Maybe we need the little fires of change in our own lives periodically to keep us less vulnerable to the major changes.

Get Off the Nail!

A neighbor saw an old dog lying on a front porch. Hearing the dog softly moaning, the neighbor approached the porch. He asked the owner why the dog was whimpering. The owner said, "He's lying on a nail." The neighbor asked, "Well, why doesn't he move?" To which the owner replied, "I guess it doesn't hurt quite that much yet."

A lot of people are like that old dog. They moan and groan about their situation but don't do anything. How bad does the pain have to get before you get up and do something else? If you are in a negative environment, take a fresh look at yourself, define where you want to be, and develop a clear plan of action for getting there.

Change, even if unwelcome, forces us to reevaluate what our best options are. Those times of transitions are great opportunities to look for recurring patterns in your life and make adjustments to build on the good and reduce the bad.

We easily become creatures of habit. A train creates a tremendous amount of momentum to keep moving along the same track. It takes an unusual or unexpected force to redirect that train. That's why, without change in some form, we are likely to simply continue on the same path.

Often in working with professionals, I am reminded of how difficult it is for them to see things in new ways. They become so accustomed to doing the same things in the same ways that any change is perceived as life-threatening, even if the current situation is frustrating or negative. They have so much training in narrow thinking that anything different is intimidating.

Dealing with Obstacles in Our Path

In ancient times, a king, wanting to test his subjects, placed a boulder in the main road leading to his city. Then he hid himself and watched to see people's reactions. Some of the king's wealthiest merchants and courtiers came by and simply walked around it. Many loudly blamed the king for not keeping the roads clear. None did anything about getting the big stone out of the way. Then a peasant came along carrying a load of vegetables. On approaching the boulder, the peasant laid down his burden and tried to move the stone to the side of the road. After much pushing and straining, he finally succeeded. As the peasant picked up his load of vegetables, he noticed a purse lying in the road where the boulder had been. The purse contained many gold coins and a note from the king indicating that the gold was for the person who removed the boulder from the road- way. The peasant learned what many others never understand. To take ini- tiative presents unexpected rewards.

> *"Obstacles are those frightful things you see when you take your eye off the goal."*
> *—Hannah More*[6]

If you ask a group of thirty second-graders, "How many of you can draw, sing, or dance?" every hand will go up as each child clamors for a chance to prove their multiple abilities. Ask the same group when they are juniors in high school and perhaps half will claim any one of these skills. Ask the same group when they're at age thirty-five, and you will find perhaps two or three who acknowledge performing adequately in any of these areas. What happened? Did they all lose their earlier abilities? No, we get used to very familiar paths in our lives and eliminate many possibilities along the way.

Much of my success as a life coach is in helping people once again see new possibilities; to peel back the layers of life and release those childhood dreams or to consider solutions they have never before considered. Unexpected change can help initiate this process.

Common Career Questions

1. *Should I find a job and stay with it until I retire?*

The average job in America for someone eighteen to forty-two years old is now 2.2 years long, and the average American worker will have fourteen to sixteen different jobs in his or her working lifetime. You must develop a sense of what you can contribute that goes beyond only one company or organization. A career path today will likely involve moving from organization to organization, creating a picture of working your way through a maze, rather than climbing a vertical ladder. In fact, a vertical rise within one organization will very likely move you away from your strongest areas of competence.

2. *Do I have to deal with change?*

Change is inevitable. It is relentless and non-discriminating. Our only choice is how we are going to respond to it. If you know your strongest competencies, are prepared, and have a clear focus, you will have a sense of continuity—not a feeling of starting over each time you are confronted with a job change.

3. *How can I keep my job from controlling my life?*

First decide what kind of life you want, then plan your work around that life. Make sure you build in balanced priorities. Exchange your time for valued priorities that go beyond just more money. Move away from the idea that more time equals more success. If you are working more than forty-five to fifty hours a week in your job (including commute time), you are limiting success in some other areas of your life. Don't expect all your fulfillment, value, and meaning to come from the work you do. Make sure you are making deposits of success in all seven areas of your life (see chapter 4).

4. *What if I don't want another corporate job? Do I have other options?*

Many people are switching to new work models. There are many varieties of work models available: consultants, freelance workers, temps, independent contractors, etc. In addition, there are many choices for businesses you can run yourself (see chapter 11).

5. *I don't have a college education. What can I do?*

Recognize that 85 percent of the reason people get promotions and opportunities in companies is due to personal skills—attitude, enthusiasm, self-discipline, and interpersonal expertise. Fifteen percent of the reason people move up is due to technical or educational skills and credentials. Today's work environment creates a level playing field. If you have the personal skills and "emotional intelligence," you can do most anything you want.

6. *My résumé has me in a rut I can't get out of. What can I do?*

Rebuild your résumé, highlighting your *transferable areas of competence* instead of just listing your job descriptions. Show your proficiency in administration, planning, sales, marketing, training, supervising, financial analysis, etc. These skills are transferable from one industry or profession to another (see chapter 6).

Dealing with Change

You may be asking yourself some tough questions:

- Is this really all there is?
- Am I doing what God wants me to do?
- Does my life have a purpose?
- Did I make a wrong turn somewhere?

Are you ready for change?

The best way to deal with the challenge of change is to be prepared to respond.

First, look at yourself. The more you understand yourself, the more you can move forward with boldness and confidence.

When you get to heaven, God is not going to ask you why you weren't more like Mother Teresa. He's likely to ask you why you weren't more like *you*. Your responsibility and source of real freedom and success is to discover who you are. Lead with your own unique talents and personality. Be authentically you and let God use you.

The power of knowing yourself acts as a compass through change. You need that changeless core, knowing how God has uniquely gifted you and what you value. With that knowledge you can forge through change with clear direction and unshakable purpose.

Finding a job is a meaningless process until you develop a clear focus that is suited to you.

Just because you have the *ability* to do something does not mean that it is well-suited to you. This is a very significant point that cannot be stressed enough. Many people have been misdirected because they had the ability to do something well. At this stage in your life, you probably have the ability to successfully do one to two hundred different things career-wise.

Dennis is a forty-three-year-old dentist. Last year he made more than $300,000. His practice is growing, and his "success" is reflected in his beautiful house and the vacations he and his family take. However, he is also being treated for depression and is increasingly overtaken by panic attacks and the dread of going to the office. In working through this process, we discovered that while Dennis has the ability to be a dentist, he is living out his parents' dream, not his own. He has now sold his dental practice and has gone back to school to get his degree in family counseling.

Genius is the ability to clearly visualize the objective.

"All Beginnings Are Hopeful!"

This is actually a quote from the president of Oxford University, spoken to entering freshman in 1944 in the midst of a world war. In coaching people going through change, I am often struck by their discouragement, frustration, and resentment. I have come to recognize, however, that those feelings reveal that the person is looking backward—at something that has already occurred. As soon as we are able to create a clear plan for the future, those feelings dissipate and are replaced by hope, optimism, and enthusiasm. In all my years of coaching, I have never seen a person who has a clear plan and goals for the future who is also depressed. They just don't go together.

Viktor Frankl, in his wonderful little book *Man's Search for Meaning*, relates his observations of people in German concentration camps. Age, health, education, or ability could not predict who would survive the atrocities there. Rather it was attitude—only those who believed that there was something better coming tomorrow were able to survive and ultimately walk away from those camps.[7]

Feeling discouraged? Miserable in your job? Just lost your business? Give yourself a new beginning tomorrow. All beginnings are hopeful. And yes, companies are waiting to hire you—if you are a person they want on their team.

Countdown to Work I Love

1. Respond to the statement, "All progress requires change, but not all change is progress."

2. Have you guaranteed your job security?

3. What do you think the "shelf life" of your diploma is?

4. What in your training or experience makes you "employable"? What value do you bring to the table—whether or not you have a degree?

5. Have you experienced any "failure" in your career? If so, what did it lead to?

6. What were your childhood goals and ambitions for life? Which ones have you been able to fulfill?

7. Who are two or three people you know who seem to have accomplished their dreams? What do you remember about their accomplishments?

8. What do you imagine your retirement will be like?

Visit www.48Days.com/worksheets for more on being a person others know, like, and trust.

Chapter 3

Yes, I Do Have an "Education"

Two roads diverged in a yellow wood,
And sorry I could not travel both
And be one traveler, long I stood
And looked down one as far as I could
To where it bent in the undergrowth;
Then took the other, as just as fair,
And having perhaps the better claim,
Because it was grassy and wanted wear;
Though as for that, the passing there
Had worn them really about the same,
And both that morning equally lay
In leaves no step had trodden black.
Oh, I marked the first for another day!
Yet knowing how way leads on to way,
I doubted if I should ever come back.
I shall be telling this with a sigh
Somewhere ages and ages hence:
Two roads diverged in a wood, and I,
I took the one less traveled by,
And that has made all the difference.
> —ROBERT FROST, "THE ROAD NOT TAKEN"

43

Nick grew up in Columbus, Ohio, in a family where Dad was an attorney and Mom was a teacher. He's never had a job because his parents wanted him to focus on his school work. They hired a coach to help him prepare for his SAT and to the delight of everyone he was accepted at a prestigious Ivy League university where he got a 3.7 GPA and a BA in English. He's now looking for a job.

Chuck also grew up on the outskirts of Columbus, Ohio. His mom was single so he hustled ways to make money since he was six years old, delivering fliers in the neighborhood, then washing and waxing neighbors' cars, making and selling his own brand of slushie, and then being the top pizza delivery guy as soon as he was old enough to drive. He struggled in school but at seventeen his talent as a bicycle racer garnered him a spot on the BMC Racing team where he trained and traveled internationally.

Both Nick and Chuck are now twenty-two years old and looking for jobs. If you had a growing company, who would you want on your team?

Does Nick have an "education" while Chuck does not?

Our ideas about education are being rocked. Major companies are moving away from a focus on SATs, GPAs, brand-name schools, and credentials. Instead, they are looking at how does this person think, solve problems, lead, and handle failure. Reflect back on how "learning" took place even twenty years ago. You spent time with the same people week after week. Depending on where you lived, that may include the gas station attendant, the local grocery store owner, your parents, a teacher or two, and the neighborhood kids who were your friends. "Learning" took place in school with the one teacher responsible for your class. If you were a privileged family, you may have been lucky enough to have an Encyclopedia Britannica set in your house—opening you up to a vast amount of information. The choices after high school were clear. If you wanted an "education," you went to the place where they controlled additional information—college. Colleges had big libraries with the books and research studies not available to the small-town students. Few people had the opportunity to go to college as it was expensive and required another four years outside the workforce. It was clear that college graduates had more access to knowledge and information and ultimately got better jobs and incomes. Thus the apparent causation was obvious: if you want a better job and more income, you must go to college and get a degree.

What Does It Mean to Be "Educated"?

But what does that look like today? Colleges became big business with dormitories, libraries, and sports stadiums to fund and support. More students were necessary to carry the ongoing costs of the institutions themselves. Standards of excellence were lowered to attract and keep more students. Thus the unique value of a college degree became diminished. But during that time our access to that privileged information has changed dramatically. Many of us now carry some form of a device in our pocket that provides us instant access to that entire compilation of human knowledge and allows us to communicate with the intellectually and economically elite anywhere in the world. If you are a poor child from Alabama, a daughter of upper income New York City parents, or one of eleven children in a family living as squatters in Nairobi, Kenya, you have access to that abundance of stored and daily developing information.

No longer is it a unique privilege to have access to that information and no longer is it necessary to study and learn and memorize what is so instantly available. Want to know the capital of Ukraine? Simply speak the question into your phone and get the answer instantly. Need to know the square root of 3,456? It doesn't take some complicated paper process—anyone can access the answer of 58.79 immediately. This is not some gradual improvement or opportunity. This is an amazing, disruptive, transforming leap forward—with immense implications for "education."

If employers know that anyone has access to the brightest minds in the world and the smartest person is not the one who has memorized the most information, then what are they looking for in potential team members today? Have you ever seen the term "equivalent experience" in a job posting? That's a nice term for saying it's really not important how you became qualified in what we're looking for, we just want to know you can bring value to our organization. We don't really care about those letters after your name if you can prove you can do the job well. The key issue is "competence," not degrees.

Colleges are no longer the only place where education occurs. The dictionary defines "education" as the act or process of imparting or acquiring general knowledge, developing the powers of reasoning and judgment, and generally of preparing oneself or others intellectually for mature life.[1] Education in the broadest sense is any experience or accumulation of knowledge that has a formative effect on the mind, spirit, character, or physical ability of an individual. The word *education* is derived from *educare* (Latin), which means to "bring up," "bring out," or "bring forth what is within." I'm confident you have had many experiences that have helped you accomplish those results. Education is an ongoing process. It certainly does not begin or end with the completion of any academic program.

> *"I have never let my schooling interfere with my education."*
> —Mark Twain

Continual learning is the key to continual living. If you stop learning you have effectively stopped living. Fortunately, we are presented with opportunities every day to learn and improve ourselves. And that improvement opens the door to new work, career, and business applications.

Going to college is not the primary determinant of whether or not you are "educated." We each must take responsibility for our own education and be prepared to prove our competence as a result. Gone are the days when companies valued credentials more than competence.

My Education Journey

Yes, I adamantly maintain that each of us needs an "education." But that occurs in many, many ways. When my oldest son

Kevin was racing bicycles professionally in Europe as an eighteen-year-old, people would ask me if I was concerned that he wasn't in college. My reply was that he may choose to get a degree someday but right then he was too busy getting an education to stop and go to college. Are you kidding me? Do you think maybe that traveling internationally would be adding knowledge, information, and education that would equal or surpass sitting in a classroom regurgitating textbook facts?

And the exciting thing is that in taking responsibility for our education today we are offered many, many options.

And no, don't assume I am throwing out the idea of college. I think it's the best choice for many people. I saw it as my best option for giving me choices other than staying on the farm. Milking cows at 5:30 a.m. on bitter cold Ohio mornings and throwing hay bales in the heat of the summer caused me to evaluate my options for other kinds of work. We didn't have radio or TV in our house, I went to a tiny rural school, our family did not own an encyclopedia set, and the little library in our town had only a few donated books. I valued the varied exposure to mechanics, plumbing, carpentry, electrical, woodworking, and agriculture gained in that lifestyle; but I saw the life of those who wore nice clothes daily and worked indoors and knew I wanted to expand my horizons.

I have always enjoyed learning. But my education has come in a constant stream; sometimes added to by being in a classroom but mostly by taking advantage of the multitude of learning and enriching opportunities offered all around us.

With no radio or TV in the house, I found my information in books and became an avid reader. Torn between the need to provide for our family and the desire to embrace his spiritual calling, my father worked both as a farmer and as pastor to the little local Mennonite church. While he was sincere about being honorable and godly, I saw that his career choices were

> *"Formal education will make you a living; self-education will make you a fortune." —Jim Rohn*

not based on authentic fit, but simply on duty and obligation. His example instilled in me the idea that work was just a necessary evil, and the only learning or education required was that necessary for basic farming success. The realities of that life left little time for anything playful or pleasurable. Frankly, anything that provided enjoyment was suspected of being self-serving or ungodly anyway, which further reinforced the idea that there was no merit in further learning. TV viewing, ball games, nice cars, clothes, and "higher education" were all examples of useless and dangerous activities that would likely pull a person away from what was eternally important.

Exhausting farm work was a matter of survival; education or work that you *enjoyed* demonstrated egotistical selfishness.

Despite the limitations on the things I could do or the places I could go, nothing could stop my mind from wandering. I remember well driving our little Ford tractor out in the fields, far away from anyone else, giving me time to imagine a world I had never seen. Somehow in that restricted world, when I was about twelve years old, I was able to get a copy of the little 33.3 rpm record by Earl Nightingale titled *The Strangest Secret*. On that recording I heard this gravelly voiced man say that I could be anything I wanted to be by simply changing my thinking. He talked about six words that could dramatically affect the results of my best efforts: *"We become what we think about."*[2] I recognized if that were true, the possibilities of what I could do with my life were limitless.

While this is a biblical principle ("As he thinks in his heart, so is he." Prov. 23:7 NKJV), I knew my expectations for that phrase would not be welcomed in our house. My dad would not see that as an acceptable method for seeing and having more than what our simple farming life offered. After all, *we're just a passin' through,* and wanting more opened the door to the dangers of moving away from contentment and basic godliness. I hid that little record under my mattress, bringing it out night after night to listen, dream, and imagine. And I started to plan what my life could look like if in fact my thinking led the way. Any sense of being trapped began to disappear as I saw my opportunity, and responsibility, for the direction of my life.

I continued to attend regular public school and welcomed the new worlds that books and classroom learning offered.

I became intensely curious about the world and began to explore the way things worked, how they could be made better, and what possibilities existed for change and innovation. I would take the lawn mower engine apart to see if I could improve its power and efficiency. I improvised new machines and inventions from old parts I salvaged from the local dump. I was drawn to the biblical stories of Joshua, Joseph, and Solomon, seeing them as examples of people who dreamed things others thought impossible and created plans of action to make their dreams a reality.

I became adept at coming up with new solutions to problems in my little world. The farming environment did provide exposure to carpentry, plumbing, electrical, and mechanical systems, but I began to recognize new opportunities all around me. I could take orders for Christmas cards and experience the thrill of "profits." Seeing the harsh conditions of our gravel road, I offered to clean and wax our neighbors' cars as one of my first businesses. Seeing our garden overflowing with produce prompted other ideas. After my mother canned all the sweet corn our cellars would hold, I would get up at five o'clock in the morning, go out and pick the remaining corn, and head for the main road with our little tractor and a trailer full of excess corn. With my homemade sign, I would sell ears of corn for thirty cents a dozen and collect my growing nest egg.

My first car did not appear because Dad took me into town and wrote a check. No, when I was eighteen years old, I purchased a 1931 Model A Ford body for fifty dollars. Learning as I went, I slowly began to build a running street rod. The meager earnings from my little businesses were poured into one piece at a time to create a road-worthy and attention-getting car. Every time I found myself with an extra five dollars, instead of blowing it on candy or clothes, I would go to the junkyard and buy a generator or a set of seats. I learned by doing, as well as by listening and talking to anyone who knew more than I did.

In our family, cars were strictly for transportation. Anything that looked "cool" or accented visual appeal or high performance was nothing but "worldly." Our cars were always black and even then we seemed to feel guilty for having one. I, on the other hand, loved seeing the bright fast cars in our periodic trips into town. After more than a year of knuckle-breaking work in an old unheated chicken coop, I drove out with an eye-popping '31 coupe with a Chrysler hemi engine. Although a simple farm kid, I had learned what was necessary to build a car that outshone those of most of my friends.

Seeing that I could think, imagine, and act my dreams into reality fueled my desire for new experiences and more self-education. Upon completing high school, the clear family expectations were that I would become a full-time part of the farming operation. It was an obligation based on doing what was responsible—and to repay for the years of having a roof over my head and food on the table. But I wanted more, and I knew that college would help open new doors for me. Against my father's wishes, I decided to pursue college classes. I was still required to help with the dairy and farming chores beginning at 5:30 a.m. But I didn't let that little detail deter me. I enrolled in a branch campus of The Ohio State University, where I could attend classes from 6:00 to 10:00 p.m.

I chose psychology as my area of major. Not because I thought that would be the beginning of an exciting career path but simply because I was interested in understanding why we do the things we do. Upon completion of my BA at The Ohio State University, I applied for one prime job as an adjunctive therapist at a prestigious psychiatric hospital. After an enjoyable four years I again was experiencing the itch to broaden my options. I had learned a great deal in that position and will be forever grateful for the psychiatrists and other therapists who taught me so willingly. They gave me a going-away party and a beautiful briefcase as I entered graduate school for yet another educational experience. My wife Joanne and I lived in an old house with our little boy where I traded my remodeling skills in lieu of rent. My assistantship eliminated tuition fees and we lived on essentially the $200 per month stipend I received for teaching Introductory Psychology to college freshmen. Joanne also sewed beautiful tailor-made clothing for hard-to-fit women, allowing us to complete this chapter of our lives with no student loan debt. Incidentally, being a teacher in the classroom terrified me initially. I enrolled in the Dale Carnegie Human Relations course to help me with my confidence and public speaking. That help was so profound I volunteered to be an assistant with them and had the privilege of continuing to go through the course many more times.

To complete the requirements for my MA in Psychology, I was required to write a Master's thesis. You know the drill. I did the research, wrote a thesis that was read by five people, and they gave me a nice certificate that hangs on my wall. Did that prove my competence as a "psychologist" or "therapist"? Not at all. But I had completed the requirements of that "educational" program and I was on my way.

After working approximately three months as a therapist at The Center for Human Understanding (how's that for a grandiose title?) in Tustin, California, I realized I was bored out of my mind sitting in a chair listening to rich kids' problems. I quickly left and reverted back to all those skills learned on the farm to provide handyman services to a ready audience in southern California. I've never been concerned about having the ability to provide income because I have had so many enriching experiences that prepared me with plenty of marketable skills. Few of those came from sitting in a seat in a classroom.

After a short time of installing ceiling fans, mowing yards, repairing toilets, washing windows, and painting houses, I joined a friend in his used car business. It was a great relationship. He purchased the cars, reconditioned them, brought them back to the lot on a prime location in Anaheim, California, where I was responsible for selling them. Yes, some family members questioned how I could "walk away" from my recently acquired master's degree. But did I really walk away?

Preparation for Real Life

How does education prepare us for real-life opportunities? Did my preparation at that point position me only for being a traditional counselor or therapist? Was my only option to sit in a chair with one person sitting across from me telling me how miserable they were? Let's think about my role in selling used cars. Is it possible I still used my "education" at that point? In my first month of selling cars I had a young man walk on to the lot dressed casually in a well-worn T-shirt. Any experienced salesman would have prejudged him with confidence that he was not a serious buyer worthy of any investment of time. He did not currently even own a car, he was dressed poorly, and he spoke with difficulty. But I had learned how to listen, how to express empathy, and to accept a person "unconditionally." So I talked to this guy and showed him anything he was interested in. He was quickly drawn to a really beautiful Corvette. Of course, wouldn't anyone be attracted to something out of their reach? He asked if he could take it for a test drive, and after verifying he did have a driver's license I agreed to take a ride with him driving. When we came back and I asked how he would be paying for the car if he decided to purchase it, he assured me he would just pay for it. While still unsure where this was going I took him in the office, wrote up a quick agreement and turned it around for him to sign. He signed his name, stood up, pulled his T-shirt up, and began pulling out stacks of $20 bills. He paid the entire amount in cash on the spot. But here's where it gets even more interesting. In the next twelve months, when you count brothers, sisters, aunts and uncles, cousins and nephews, I sold fourteen cars to that one extended family. All because I treated one young man with courtesy, respect, and interest. Did I "use" my degree in psychology?

Several years later I decided to study for my doctorate. I enrolled in classes and eagerly immersed myself in the process of formalized study once again. I completed the entire program with flying colors. Then I met with my dissertation committee. Four very old guys met with me to outline the process. Having been through a similar scenario with my earlier degrees, I simply asked for clarification. A doctoral dissertation is not meant for reading by the common person. It must be written in a "scholarly" fashion with countless footnotes and references to other works. Upon completion it would be read by these same four guys who would then hopefully give me yet another really nice piece of paper to hang on my wall.

At that point I summarized the options as I saw them: (1) I could spend the next two years researching and writing that cumbersome document so these old guys would be impressed enough to give me that piece of paper, or (2) I could spend that same amount of time and effort researching and writing a book that would be readable by the average person and hopefully make a million dollars or so as a result. Much to the chagrin of those four old guys, I chose option #2. The resulting book was the original edition of *48 Days to the Work You Love* and it has done exactly what I intended.

But doing what I intended did not happen by accident. I had observed that best-selling authors were very involved in the *selling* process. So I researched and went to a MegaBook University event with Mark Victor Hansen (coauthor of *Chicken Soup for the Soul*) in Los Angeles. For three days Joanne and I sat and listened to Mark and his guests share about how to generate sales for our books. I came back to Tennessee, did what he suggested, and in the next three years took in more than $2 million selling my little 3-ring binder version of *48 Days to the Work You Love*—before I ever talked to a traditional publisher.

So Where Did I Get My Education?

Remember that little audio recording I mentioned, *The Strangest Secret*? The impact of that message continued to shape my life and choices. That recording became the first product of the company called Nightingale Conant, and they went on to produce hundreds of inspirational programs with those I call the masters of achievement. I became an avid customer, purchasing hundreds of programs like *Lead the Field, The Psychology of Winning, How to Get Rich in America, See You at the Top, The Science of Personal*

Achievement, and *Seeds of Greatness.* I attended seminars and work-shops by those same authors and sought out new ones like Launch, EntreLeadership, Social Media Marketing World, LeaderCast, Experts Academy, and more. One of the highlights of my life was when the folks at Nightingale Conant contacted me a few years ago. I had never talked to them and was simply a loyal customer. But they said they had purchased my materials, had tested them on their audience, and wanted me to come to Chicago and create a six-hour audio program using my principles that we would call *Dream Job.* It was a thrill to work with them in that process and to be included in that amazing group of masters of achievement. (And *Dream Job* is now the third highest ranked program, based on customer feedback, in the entire Nightingale Conant product line.)

I've continued my lifelong love of reading, listening, and learn-ing. Years ago I made it a practice to spend at least two hours daily listening to, or reading, positive materials. That practice has given me access to the greatest thinkers of the world and an ongoing education that is current, practical, and tied directly to generating income in my business. My primary activities now are writing, speaking, and coaching. Yet I've never had a class on writing, speaking, or coaching as any part of my academic degree pro-grams. I've never had a business class although today my business allows me a lifestyle enjoyed by very few people.

I value having grown up on the farm. I loved the times I spent in the classroom. I loved that time of selling cars. I loved the time following that where I had an auto accessory business, a health and fitness center, a sales training organization, and the opportunities I've had in coaching, speaking, and writing. No one piece of "edu-cation" prepared me for the rich opportunities I experience today.

I have always loved the process of study—because my goal was to get the knowledge and learning—not to get a piece of paper with my name on it. I have always viewed "education" as something that helps increase my options, broadens my horizons, and perhaps positions me as an expert in a given field. Framing it as such, one can easily see that "education" can occur in many, many ways. Sitting in a classroom with thirty-two other people, regurgitating information fed from the professor may in fact be one of the poorer methods of becoming educated.

So where do you think I got my "education"? If I depended on my academic degrees, would I really be qualified to write, speak, and coach?

What life experiences are part of your "education"?

Ten Steps to Education

Here are ten steps to education. These are things you can do this year to open the floodgates of new opportunity and new wealth.

1. *Read (or listen to) at least twelve great books.* I have an Amazon.com Prime membership with unlimited Free Two-Day Shipping. I buy books liberally and encourage you to do the same. Want to know what books I recommend? See a complete list at www.48days.com/reading.

> "The man who doesn't read good books has no advantage over the man who can't read them." —Mark Twain

2. *Attend three or four seminars.* Choose what you'd like but go with an open mind. I attend a lot of seminars each year. My goal is not to change my life with any ONE seminar, but to learn at least one great idea that I can use.

> "Man's mind, once stretched by a new idea, never regains its original dimensions." —Oliver Wendell Holmes

3. *Work on improving your Emotional Intelligence.* Emotional Intelligence (EQ) is the ability to use and manage your emotions in positive ways to relieve stress, communicate effectively, overcome challenges, and defuse conflict. Your skill in this area will allow you to form healthier relationships, achieve greater success at work, and lead a more fulfilling life.

> "Learning is a treasure that will follow its owner everywhere." —Chinese Proverb

4. *Listen to three or four informational on-demand radio programs and read three or four blogs each week.* You may be an audio or print learner. No right or wrong—just select what works for you. The free information is priceless.

> "The man who is too old to learn was probably always too old to learn." —Henry S. Haskins[3]

5. *Take two or three courses in areas of interest.* You don't have to be "accepted" or lock in thousands of dollars in tuition. Just explore the many courses that can give you marketable skills on sites like:

- www.khanacademy.org
- www.lynda.com
- www.vtc.com
- www.udemy.com

These sites have thousands of professional video courses covering almost every topic imaginable. You can gain access to all courses on the site for a small monthly fee or a small fee for the individual course. Many of these courses have certificates of completion to show adequate preparation for work in that area. More and more employers are accepting these certificates as proof of training.

> "If you're not prepared to be wrong you'll never come up with something original." —Sir Ken Robinson[4]

6. *Reach out to help someone else.* There are people all around the world who are committed to living a better story. Helping them will help you feel connected to a larger life than what you have now.

7. *Acquire at least one new skill this year.* Each year I select an area of interest having nothing to do with business or making money. Purely for the "education." Imagine that. You may want to learn a new language, explore a musical instrument, or take up bird watching. The stretch will add to your life in unexpected ways.

"Anyone who stops learning is old, whether at twenty or eighty." —Henry Ford[5]

8. *Become comfortable with your presentation skills.* No matter what your career or business, you must be comfortable presenting your ideas. It will do wonders for your confidence and self-esteem. You will find it easier to complete a sales transaction, have conversations with family and friends, and find success in your career.

9. *Design your own health and fitness program.* Success is never just about making money. If you deplete your physical resources, you will fail at everything else. Make sure you are making deposits of success in this area every day.

10. *Plan two trips this year.*

- Visit a popular tourist destination during the off-season (Chicago at Christmas time).
- You can swap houses with someone anywhere in the world. See www.homeexchange.com or www.homelink.org for ideas.
- You can rent a unique place from the owner, like a cottage in Ireland for $280 a week. (Vacation Rentals by Owner: www.vrbo.com)

I'm sure you could probably add more examples of experiences in your life that have helped you get an "education." With today's technology you can listen to inspirational, uplifting material while cleaning the house or driving your car. (Speaking of driving time—join the Automobile University. If you drive twenty-five thousand miles a year at an average speed of 46 mph, you will spend about the same amount of time in your car as an average college student spends in the classroom. The question then is, what are you doing with that time? You can listen to any one of thousands of programs and transform your success.) You can take a long nature walk and really see your surroundings. I often take a walk on our property with coaching clients. If that person misses the squirrels, the deer, the butterflies, the waterfall, and the setting sun, it gives me a pretty clear picture of why they are also unconnected socially, physically, and spiritually.

100 Percent College Admission—How Sad

One Sunday on a leisurely drive back from lunch we passed one of the most prestigious private high schools in our area. A sign was proudly posted at the front entrance stating: "100% College Admission for Our Seniors—Again."

I'll have to admit I cringed on seeing that. Now I know that any high school principal who doesn't claim this as his or her goal is likely to be accused of not having the students' best interests at heart and would also likely be run out of town by indignant parents. But personally, I think there is a major elitism at play here. And ultimately, a lot of those students suffer as a result. Is our goal really to prepare every student for life in a cubicle? In looking at my grandchildren I see those for whom I would weep at such a prospect.

The elitism is in believing that every occupation pursued by a path outside of college is somehow "lower" and not a worthy pursuit for serious students. We have become a culture that looks down on labor and craftsman positions. So, really, in this graduating class we will have no Ferrari mechanics, no sculptors, no HVAC specialists, no one I can contact to design another water feature, no skilled carpenters, no stonemasons, no welders, and no piano tuners?

In the spring of this year I had a young man come out to do a normal check-up on our air conditioning systems. Just a check-up, no parts were required. He was here less than two hours and my bill was $149. A few days later my John Deere tractor was returned with new bearings in the front wheels. Total bill—$2,690.78. Most of that was labor, billed at $70 an hour. At the same time I know a

> *"An educational system isn't worth a great deal if it teaches young people how to make a living but doesn't teach them how to make a life."*
> *—Author Unknown*

young attorney who is working part-time at Kinkos at $10 an hour to supplement his income. The HVAC guy and tractor mechanic are banking $70 an hour.

In 1943, Joseph Schumpeter wrote that the expansion of "higher education" beyond what our labor market demands creates for white-collar workers "employment in substandard work or at wages below those of the better-paid manual workers." And then he added, "it may create unemployability of a particularly disconcerting type. The man who has gone to college or university easily becomes *psychically unemployable* in manual occupations without necessarily acquiring employability in professional work."[6] I'm sure you know people who are stuck in $12 an hour jobs who would never lower themselves to work in something like being a tractor mechanic.

Sir Ken Robinson, who has made the study of creativity in schools his life's work, says that instead of fueling creativity and imagination, our educational systems are actually stifling those. In one of the most popular and humorous TED talks in history he said, "We have sold ourselves into a fast-food model of education, and it's impoverishing our spirit and our energies as much as fast food is depleting our physical bodies. . . . Imagination is the source of every form of human achievement. And it's the one thing that I believe we are systematically jeopardizing in the way we educate our children and ourselves."[7]

If we value the innate abilities of our children and really want the best for them, should we not encourage their creativity and imagination and consider a broad range of occupational possibilities?

I must admit I've made a very good living working with people who at forty-five years of age admit they are living someone else's dream. As we unpack that incongruity and begin to move toward an authentic life, all kinds of things come to the surface as meaningful work possibilities. Pastors become artists, dentists become forest rangers, and doctors become organic gardeners.

Having the *ability* to go to college is not enough reason for doing so. There must be more of an alignment with a person's values, dreams, and passions. I have worked with countless professionals who have proven their academic *ability* to create a life they detest.

Many of us have been concerned about companies' liberal use of outsourcing. Many of the jobs college students trained for can now easily be outsourced to China, Taiwan, or India. However, if I need my roof repaired, drain unclogged, lawn mowed, or want another beautiful sculpture from a standing tree on my property, I can't have someone in China provide that service. People with those skills are immune from outsourcing. Or as has been said, "You can't hammer a nail over the Internet."[8]

Let's stop depriving our children of their best options. I'd like to see that sign say—60 percent college, 10 percent trade school, 10 percent continuing family business, 10 percent entrepreneurs, and 10 percent world travel to further clarify a career path. That would make me want to send my child there.

Would you agree that a goal of 100 percent college admission for any high school class is ridiculous?

 Reader Comment

"I am considered a college dropout by most people I talk to about education. I have an AA transfer degree. I have some people tell me about their BA and how they worked hard for four to seven years and graduated with honors. Then I usually point out the spot they missed cleaning the toilet. I train all of the commercial cleaners for a cleaning company in Springfield, MO (a relatively big college town in MO) and have run across a lot of graduates that regret their degrees. Their solutions tend to lean toward going back to school to get another degree, as if they think the problem is with their career choice, and not their career preparation. For a miniscule fraction of the cost of just the books required for one year of college, an "informal student" can get the tools to find their passion, study it, and in some cases, start a business around it and market that business. Which option sounds better to you?" —Ryan

---

Beyond Humiliated—Stuck in Sameness

I saw a news item where a gentleman has been taking a ninety-minute train ride into New York each day, where he walked the streets wearing a sandwich board sign which read, "Almost homeless; looking for employment. Very experienced operations and administration manager."

He said he was beyond the point of being humiliated—he just needed a job. He said, "When you're out of work and you face having nothing—I mean, having no income—pride doesn't mean anything. I have to take care of my family." His résumé included thirty-six years in the toy industry before being laid off eight months earlier.

I know this is an all-too-common feeling for lots of people. Hey, I'm an old farm kid. If the cow is old and has stopped giving milk, standing there begging for more milk is probably not a good solution. I'd be out looking for something new to quench my thirst. Predictions are that we are rapidly reaching the time when only 50 percent of the American workforce will be "employees." The rest will be contingency workers, independent contractors, temps, freelance workers, consultants, entrepreneurs, electronic immigrants—and lots of other interesting descriptions that are showing up every day. Rather than trying to force the sameness of the old work models, lead the way into the new ways of working and making income.

When my dad was eighty-eight years old after retiring as a farmer, he was driving his own van, hauling Amish people to places they wanted to go. He charged $2.00 a mile and often drove five hundred miles a day, providing them with a valuable service and enjoying the time spent visiting. We've got stories coming in every day from people moving from construction to accounting, farrier to software developer, pastor to artist, cubicle to real estate sales and much more.

If you are out of work—don't wait on a paycheck. It may never come. What is it that you can do that fulfills a need someone else has? How could you provide that in a way that does not depend on a "salary"?

 Looking for Three Years

"Dan, my husband has been looking for a job for at least three years, but he seems to be having trouble getting past the hurdle of not working for that long a time. (He was the one to quit and stay at home with our first child, and, for the past few years, he has been trying to return to work.) Recently, he passed three of the four CPA exams and is going back to school for his Master's, and those activities seem to be generating some interest. However, nothing gets very far (lots of résumés sent, an interview here or there, but someone else is always hired). He has started calling places a week or two after sending a résumé, but that also does not seem to be helping very much." —Sandy

Sandy: Never confuse activity with accomplishment. This much time out of the game will play havoc with your husband's self-esteem and confidence. He's likely trying to look busy while avoiding the reality of job searching. Lots of people "go back to school" when a job search isn't going well. It's a socially acceptable way to hide out and procrastinate having to deal with creating income. It's not the economy—but these other factors that are crippling your husband. He needs to be very strategic about his job search. Start with thirty to forty target companies. Send a letter of introduction, then cover letter and résumé, then phone follow-up— that should produce five to six interviews. Of those he should receive at least two offers. If not, zero in on the area of breakdown in this practical sequence that gets results—even in today's economy.

Go to 48Days.com where the complete Job Search schedule is listed—and yes, 48 Days is a reasonable time to focus, search, and get multiple offers for work you love.

Countdown to Work I Love

1. If it's true that *"We become what we think about,"* where is your thinking taking your life?

2. How has your own reading and attending conferences increased your marketability?

3. What have you done this year to increase your Emotional Intelligence?

4. How are you expanding your creativity and imagination—right now?

5. Do you think everyone needs to go to college?

6. What life experiences have added to your "education"?

Visit www.48Days.com/worksheets for more on getting an "education" in today's world.

Chapter 4

Creating a Life Plan

Work is love made visible.
And if you cannot work with love but only with distaste,
it is better that you should leave your work and sit at the gate
of the temple and take alms of those who work with joy.
For if you bake bread with indifference, you bake a bitter
bread that feeds but half man's hunger.
And if you grudge the crushing of the grapes,
your grudge distills a poison in the wine.
And if you sing though as angels, and love not the singing,
you muffle man's ears to the voices of the day and the voices
of the night.
All work is empty save when there is love;
and when you work with love you bind yourself to yourself,
and to one another, and to God.
　　　　　　　　　　—KAHLIL GIBRAN, *THE PROPHET*

As the pastor of a small church, Rob was fulfilling the multiple duties of a pastor; he was the teacher, encourager, comforter, hospital visitor, administrator, and friend. Surely there could be no better expression of a godly "calling." Coming from a blue collar working family, Rob had the desire to make a difference, to lead people into their best lives, to be recognized in the community, and to provide financially for his wife and children. He had experienced a dramatic change in his own life and had chosen the path that seemed most obvious to help others find answers to life's biggest questions. And yet Rob was experiencing tremendous unrest. He was quick-tempered at home and frustrated with the demands of his congregation. With the meager salary provided, financial strains were constant and Rob was working as a night desk clerk at a local hotel just to add a few dollars to his income. Yet he was determined to hang on to what surely was his "calling." Don't open doors and a clear sense of doing what is right confirm the accuracy of his direction?

Or do they? How do we develop a clear sense of direction regarding our careers? Are open doors, family influence, educational opportunity, and new technologies the best determinants of our direction?

Is Your Job Your Calling?

Here's a framework for moving toward the decisions for what we do in our work. There are three words that tend to be used interchangeably—and they shouldn't be. These are vocation, career, and job. The distinctions are significant.

Vocation

Vocation is the most profound of the three, the largest concept, and it must incorporate *calling, purpose, mission,* and *destiny.* This is the big picture that many people never identify for themselves. It's what you're doing in life that makes a difference for you, that builds meaning for you, and that you can look back on in your later years to see the impact you've made on the world. Stephen Covey said we all want "to live, to love, to learn and to leave a legacy."[1] Our vocation will leave a legacy. The word *vocation* comes from the Latin *vocaré*, which means "to call." It suggests that you are listening for something that is calling out to you—something that is particular to you. A calling is something you have to listen for, attuning yourself to the message. Vocation then is not so much pursuing a goal as it is listening for a voice. Before I can tell my life what I want to do with it, I must listen for that voice telling me who I am. Vocation does not come from willfulness, but from listening.

> *VOCATION—from the Latin* vocaré, *which means, "to call"*[2]

And let me be quick to add—everyone has a vocation, or calling. It's not something reserved for a chosen few who end up as pastors, priests, missionaries, or monks. As Thomas Merton put it, "A tree gives glory to God by being a tree. For in being what God means it to be it is obeying Him."[3] In the same way, we fulfill our calling by being excellent at whatever God created us to be. Everything we do ought to be part of fulfilling our vocation.

A reader of my blog commented, "Talent is nothing to God. He only seeks a fully surrendered and obedient individual." I beg to differ. How does God "call" us except through giving us talents and abilities, personality traits and passions that draw us in a particular direction? To think God will ask a "fully surrendered and obedient individual" to do something where there is no alignment with natural talents opens the door to heartache and frustration. "Based on the gift each one has received, use it to serve others, as good managers of the varied grace of God" (1 Pet. 4:10).

I've met with too many pastors, missionaries, and teachers who were obedient and willing, but whose natural skills did not line up with their attempts to do something "godly." Many confused "calling" with the family tradition or the expectations of others. And their work was frustrating, spiritually depleting, and ultimately the trigger that led to a crisis demanding change.

When there is an alignment of our skills, abilities, talents, personality traits, and passions, we will recognize God's "call." We will have found our sweet spot and will experience work that is fulfilling, meaningful, purposeful, and profitable. For example, you may have a *vocation* or *calling* "to help reduce pain and suffering in the world." What kind of work does that translate to? Understanding *career* will help answer that question.

Career

If one looks at the derivations of the words *vocation* and *career* you will immediately get a feel for the difference between them. "Career" is the term we hear most often today. That word comes originally from the Latin word for "cart" and later from the Middle French word for "racetrack." Dictionary.com offers, "to run or move rapidly along; go at full speed."[5] In other words, you can go around and around really fast for a long time but never get anywhere. That is why in today's volatile work environment, even professionals with careers like physician, attorney, CPA, dentist, and engineer may choose to get off the expected track and choose another career. A career is a line of work, but never the only way to fulfill one's calling. You can have different careers at different points in your life. Conversely, two or three different careers can all support one's *calling*.

> *"Where the spirit does not work with the hand there is no art." —Leonardo Da Vinci*[4]

"Dan, the merry-go-round of my professional life has left me no farther than a few steps from where I got on and now with a weak stomach." Thus began the description of life from a very "successful" attorney. Many times a career path starts because of circumstances, rather than priorities. Family expectations, chance occurrences, a friendly teacher, or seeking money can lead us down an unfulfilling career path. It's tough to make good choices at eighteen that will be meaningful at forty-five. Just recently, I saw a forty-four-year-old client who opened with the comment, "I'm tired of living my life based on the decisions made by an eighteen-year-old."

> *CAREER—"to run or move at full speed, rush wildly; careen"*

If we use the example above of a vocation or calling to "help reduce pain and suffering in the world," we can now list multiple careers that would fully embrace that calling. For example, being a physician, nurse, counselor, pastor, teacher, massage therapist, scientist, politician, social entrepreneur, or writer would all have the potential to fit beautifully. Thus, we all have the freedom of changing careers at varied times in our lives, knowing we can simply review our "vocation" and find a new application for the next season of our lives.

Job—One's Daily Activities

A job is the most specific and immediate of the three terms. It has to do with one's daily activities that produce income or a paycheck. The dictionary defines *job* as "anything a person is expected or obliged to do; duty; responsibility."[6] As mentioned previously, the average job is now 2.2 years in length, meaning the average person just entering the workplace will have fourteen to sixteen different jobs in his or her working lifetime. Thus the "job" surely cannot be the critical definition of one's vocation or calling. Yet the job should in fact be one expression of that calling and an integration of one's ministry. There is a Hebrew word, *avodah*, from which comes both the words "work" and "worship."[7] To the Hebrew man, what he was doing on Thursday morning was just as much an expression of worship as being in the synagogue on the Sabbath. Nothing in Scripture depicts the Christian life as divided into sacred and secular parts. Rather, it shows a unified life, one of wholeness, in which everything we do is service to God, including our daily work, whatever that may be.

For example, if we take one career that fits a calling "to help reduce pain and suffering in the world"—nurse—and look in any city in America, we will find thousands of "jobs" available. Jobs will come and go, thus losing a job or taking the initiative to change jobs should never derail a person from the fulfillment of his or her "calling." Those inevitable times of transition are simply opportunities to take a fresh look at your preparation and positioning, and to then find a new and perhaps more fulfilling application in the next job or business venture.

The Rat Race—Improve Your Life; Think Like a Rat

We talk about "being in the rat race," but this is probably unfair. It's actually demeaning to the rats. Rats won't stay in a race when it's obvious there's no cheese. The popular little book *Who Moved My Cheese?* showed how even smart rats quickly look for new routes to follow when the cheese is gone. Humans, on the other hand, seem to often get themselves into traps from which they never escape. Some research shows that up to 70 percent of white-collar workers are unhappy with their jobs. Ironically, they are also spending more and more time working.

Jan Halper, a Palo Alto psychologist, has spent ten years exploring the careers and emotions of more than four thousand male executives. She found that 58 percent of those in middle management felt they had wasted many years of their lives struggling to achieve their goals. They were bitter about the many sacrifices they had made during those years.

Rats, however, move on once they realize the cheese is gone or perhaps was never there. Rats would probably be embarrassed to be labeled "being in the human race" for doing ridiculous things like continuing to go to a job that they hated every day.

Good career decisions have to be based on more than a casual look at the job opportunities or at one's aptitudes. What we invest our time in daily and weekly must incorporate three critical areas mentioned in the Introduction: (1) Skills and Abilities, (2) Personality Tendencies, and (3) Values, Dreams, and Passions. The most common mistake people make in choosing a career is to do something simply because they are good at it. The accountant who is good at math or the sales person who is a persuader may still be frustrated because that career forces them to be gregarious or to promote a product for which they have little enthusiasm. Remembering the happiest times in your life and the times when you felt most fulfilled are better indicators of your calling than just knowing what you have the ability to do. Circumstances alone are not good predictors of God's calling. Many people responded to circumstances early in life and at age forty-five are realizing true components of how God has created them are missing in their work.

In Rob's case we were able to identify his passion for painting beautiful works of art. However, the challenge of providing for a wife and five children seemed to make painting and creating art unrealistic or impractical, another issue that frequently misdirects people from their best callings. Fortunately, Rob was able to create a dramatic transition. For four years he did faux finishing, creating visual beauty by using brushes, sponges, and rags on the walls of people's homes and offices. That time of transition allowed him to produce the needed income for a growing family, and to establish his reputation as a credible artist.

Today, no longer a pastor and no longer doing faux finishes, he creates dramatic works of art with a musical theme. They explode with the spiritual passion with which he completes each project. He is generating eight to ten times the income he was generating previously and is able to "minister" in a way more authentic and fitting for him. He shared with me that as a pastor, people knew what to expect of him—what he would think and say. Now he is the artist, having unique opportunities to relate to many people. They openly share their hurts, frustrations, and vulnerabilities in ways they never did to the "pastor." He now understands that a church-related job is not more "godly" if it is not right for him. God gifts each of us with unique characteristics. Understanding our skills and abilities, our personality tendencies, and equally important, our values, dreams, and passions is the first step in identifying the right job.

The career or job you have does not determine the accuracy of the "fit" with your calling. Only you can know that. There must be a sense of meaning, fulfillment, peace, and accomplishment to

> *"There I advise no one to enter any religious order or the priesthood, indeed, I advise everyone against it—unless he is forearmed with this knowledge and understands that the works of monks and priests, however holy and arduous they may be, do not differ one whit in the sight of God from the works of the rustic laborer in the field or the woman going about her household tasks, but that all works are measured before God by faith alone . . . it greatly tends to hypocrisy, by reason of its outward show and unusual characters, which engenders conceit and a contempt of the common Christian life."*
> *—Martin Luther, upon noting the artificial elevation of those doing "spiritual work" and their tendency to be proud and in possession of a higher calling*

confirm that there is a proper alignment. Being a missionary in the absence of those characteristics will provide the deep desire to change and grow. Being a farmer with those attributes in place will provide confirmation that you are living out God's unique calling for your life.

 Reader Question

"As an eighteen-year-old going into college I was ill prepared to select my forever career. Now after recently graduating from college with a sizable amount of debt due to accepting career specific scholarships (that I later grew out of and now must repay), I feel as if I am still finding my passion. How do adults find their forever careers?" —Belinda

Wow, what a great question. There is no "forever career"—only a forever calling. The application

> *"And now, with God's help, I shall become myself."*
> —Søren Kierkegaard

in career can change repeatedly. Be comfortable knowing this is an ongoing process. It's a journey to be embraced, not a destination to get to quickly.

The Bible's Perspective on Work

The Bible gives dignity to any work. There are no non-sacred occupations. "Called to ministry" or "full-time service" are simply cultural misrepresentations of God's view of meaningful work. We need to eliminate the artificial ranking of the godliness of work. There are no second-class citizens in the workplace. I thank God for the talents of our lawn maintenance man and am touched deeply when I see the beauty he creates in the grass, flowers, and trees surrounding our home. And I am worn out by getting one more letter from someone who suddenly discovered they were "called into full-time service." That immediately creates the false dichotomy of those who are *called* and those who are not. Each one of us is called to "full-time service," doing work that engages our unique talents and passions. There are not "higher" callings; only "authentic" callings that fit the uniqueness of each individual.

Most Americans evaluate their lives in retrospect, having no clear sense of control, purpose, or destiny for the future. Without knowing where you are going, you are doomed to evaluate your life looking in the rearview mirror.

Here are some unsolicited but revealing statements about where people see themselves:

- fifty-one-year-old businessman: *"I feel like I've lived my whole life by accident."*
- wife of professor: *"I feel like we have been free-falling for the last thirteen years."*
- salesman: *"I feel like I'm a ball in a pinball machine."*

- fifty-six-year-old (Ph.D. in Theology currently driving a bus): *"I feel like I've been given six seconds to sing, and I'm singing the wrong song."*
- fifty-three-year-old businessman: *"I feel like my life is a movie that's almost over, and I haven't even bought the popcorn yet."*
- collection agent: *"I've lived my life up until now as though driving with the parking brake on."*
- forty-six-year-old "successful" car salesman: *"I feel like a lost ball in tall cotton."*
- thirty-nine-year-old automotive engineer: *"I'm a butterfly caught in a spider's web, with my life slowly being sucked out."*
- twenty-seven-year-old computer specialist: *"I'm a box of parts and nothing fits together."*
- thirty-one-year-old attorney: *"Law school sucked all the life and creativity out of me."*
- fifty-five-year-old dentist: *"Failing in my practice knocked the wind out of my sails. Still waiting for a breeze to bring me in."*

These are frequent feelings among even "successful" people. It is quite common and healthy to at any point in life, draw a line in the sand and take a fresh look at who you are, what you are doing, and where you want to go.

 Learning to Get Back Up

Within a few seconds of when it is born, a baby giraffe struggles to its feet. Shortly afterward, however, the mother will knock it over from its wobbly stance. This process is repeated each time the baby struggles to its feet until the young giraffe has the strength to stand on its own without falling. What seems like an unkind act is of vital importance to the survival of the young animal. It is, in fact, an act of love by the mother for its child. For the baby giraffe, the world is a dangerous place, and it must learn without delay how to quickly get back on its feet.

The late Irving Stone, who spent a lifetime studying the lives of great men such as Michelangelo,
Vincent van Gogh, and others, noted a common characteristic of all great men: "You cannot destroy these
people," he said. "Every time they're knocked down,
they stand up."[8]

Perhaps the unwelcome event you've encountered
is just an opportunity to help you know how to stand
up stronger.

—————————

A clear sense of purpose will provide a feeling of continuity
and contentment to carry you through the inevitable changes of a
volatile workplace. Developing a clear focus leads to confidence,
boldness, and enthusiasm in living. If you cannot visualize what
you want the future to be, you are likely to end up feeling like a
victim of circumstances. Don't say you never had a chance if you
can't define what success would look like for you. If you know
where you are going, you can respond to *priorities* rather than *circumstances* and create the future you want.

Develop a long-term perspective; don't be like the farmer in
Aesop's fable *The Goose and the Golden Egg*. The farmer, having
become impatient with getting only one golden egg a day, decided
to cut the goose open and get all the eggs at once. Obviously, not
understanding the anatomy of a goose, he cut off the opportunity
to get any more golden eggs. We are in a society that emphasizes
instant everything: text messages, cell phones, and instant coffee.
Real personal success seldom comes in that instant fashion but
rather by careful planning for the long-term future.

When we talk about success, we are talking about more areas
of life than just a career. Too many people have sacrificed success
in physical, family, spiritual, and social areas in their attempts for
success in their careers. Stay committed to achieving success in
multiple areas of your life. You don't have to choose—you can have
it all. (More to come on that topic in chapter 5.)

"A Man with a Toothache"

Shakespeare once stated, "A man with a toothache cannot be in love," meaning simply that the attention demanded by the toothache doesn't allow him to notice anything other than his pain. In working with people going through job change, I often find Shakespeare's principle to be confirmed. I see grown men ignoring their wives, hiding out to avoid seeing their friends, watching too much TV, and eating foods that numb their minds. I see women embarrassed about yet another layoff stop going to church, spend money they do not have, read romance novels rather than inspirational material, and snap at their kids when asked an innocent question. The "pain" of the job needs seem to mask the health, vitality, and success they have in other life areas.

Going through job change provides a great opportunity to take a fresh look at your success in other areas. It's an opportunity not to diminish but to make additional deposits of success in your physical well-being. The energy and creativity that can come from a sharp mind and body can generate the very ideas you need at this time. Pick up a pizza rather than an expensive dinner and enjoy the extra family time together. Organize a pot luck supper with a group of your friends—you'll be surprised how many of them are going through a similar experience and providing one dish will cost you no more than eating your own meal. Pick up a great book to read. If you read only ten minutes a day, you can read a new book a month—and that can transform your insight and preparation for new options. Stay connected spiritually. You'll realize that in the scope of eternity, this event is probably a tiny spot on the time line.

Our common American work model has been:

In this model, the job is central. We are frequently more defined by *what we do* than by *who we are*. When meeting a new person, the conversation normally goes as follows: *"Hi, John, I'm Dan. What do you do?"* From that one brief answer, we make conclusions about that person's intelligence, education, income, and value to society. With this model, we get our total sense of worth from our work. All other aspects of our lives are forced to fit in around the job, if there is time. This leads to resentment, frustration, feelings of loss of control, and lack of balance. It also leaves one very vulnerable in that if something happens to that job, whether by circumstances or by your own choice, then the question becomes, *"Who am I?"* That is what happens when your total identity and sense of worth are in your job.

What we need is a paradigm shift to:

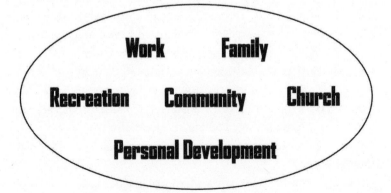

Yes, your *job/work/vocation/career* has to incorporate how God has gifted you, what you want to accomplish, and how you want to be remembered. However, you need success equally in those other areas as well. You need a life plan that integrates work with the equally important components of a successful life. While important, we need to remember that a job is simply ONE tool for a successful life.

Next time you meet someone, try asking, "How are you making the world a better place?" rather than the normal, "What do you do?"

Our goal should be to plan our *work* around our *life*, rather than planning our *life* around our *work*. You know how it typically goes: Dad gets a job offer in some remote city six states away and immediately uproots the family from school, friends, and community to secure that one artificially magnified piece of "success." Often the sacrifices made in other areas leave unanticipated wounds in other family members. I suggest determining the ideal life first, including where that would be geographically, with the full confidence that meaningful work can be found (or created) anywhere you may choose to live.

Looking at areas other than career can help you develop clear patterns and commonalities that then help define what your job/work/vocation/career ought to be. This really is a reverse process but one that leads to true fulfillment. Too often, people choose a career or line of work because Uncle Bob did it or because they heard you could make a lot of money doing it.

 ### I Just Work for the Money

"I've never been happy practicing law." "I have never had a sense of purpose." "I feel destined to do something great, but have no idea why or what." "I work only for the money."

These are statements from a young attorney—who in his last position had been sick for six months, "triggered initially by stress." But a new "career opportunity" presented itself and he is now working in a prestigious position with a Fortune 500 company. Unfortunately, the sickness is returning, starting with the symptoms of a choking feeling and shortness of breath.

We've said it before, but money is never enough compensation for investing our time and energy. There must be a sense of meaning, purpose, and accomplishment. Anything that does not blend our values, dreams, and passions will cause us on some level, to choke. A life well lived must go beyond just making a paycheck—even if it's a very large one.

The Bible tells us in Ecclesiastes 5:10, "The one who loves money is never satisfied with money, and whoever loves wealth is never satisfied with income. This too is futile." If money is the only reward of your job, you will begin to see deterioration in other areas of your life—physically, emotionally, spiritually, and in your relationships.

Proper alignment in doing work we love does not mean our families will be eating rice and beans. In fact, proper alignment releases not only a sense of peace and accomplishment, but money is likely to show up in unexpected ways. I have been amazed at seeing deposits in my account as a result of recommending great conferences to my readers and then getting referral commissions as well.

In summary:

- Recognize that your career is not your whole life. It is simply one tool for a successful life.
- Don't put all your energies into one area. Be committed to achieving success in all areas of life.
- Our physical health has a direct relationship to the energy and creativity we bring to our work.
- Proper career alignment will directly affect our finances.
- Our success in finances and the other areas will never far exceed our personal and spiritual development.

> *"Success is never an accident. It typically starts as imagination, becomes a dream, stimulates a goal, grows into a plan of action— which then inevitably meets with opportunity. Don't get stuck along the way." —Dan Miller*

 "Fire in the Belly"

James wrote, "I find it constantly challenging to tie a creative based lifestyle together with financial security. Personally, I struggle to stay true to my creativity and not to cave to my fear of security. I am constantly searching for that inspiration that ties my life together. Yes, inspiration. I know that I have God's Spirit running through me and that each move of my life is guided. To fall back on that faith and move forward is the challenge I face. I have faced it and get by, but it is definitely a work of faith. I just need to not lose sight of the 'fire in the belly' that empowers it all. This is true, both spiritually, physically, and mentally. Teach me to have faith in my own existence."

James—yes, hang on to that "fire in the belly." Too many people ignore that fire in order to be *practical* and *realistic* and end up trying to do something they don't enjoy. You can be creative, artistic, and innovative and still generate extraordinary income. Here's an example: We are told that 95 percent of authors never make more than $40,000 a year. So if I want to make much more than that I have to look for ways to do what 95 percent of authors are not doing. I can take my core message and present it in traditional books, but I can also share that message through audio compilations, instructional manuals, live events, affiliate programs, speaking engagements, eBooks, online courses, and membership groups and quickly put myself in the 5 percent category. If you are an artist, sculptor, photographer, interior designer, musician, athlete, comedian, or stay-at-home mom, you can do the same. Just look for the things that 95 percent of the others in that area are not willing to do—and you will bypass the financial lack commonly expected in your area of expertise.

A clear plan of action will separate you from 97 percent of the people you meet. Everyone has dreams, but very few ever turn those into goals. The difference between a dream and a goal is that a goal has a time line of action laid out.

Countdown to Work I Love

1. In today's rapidly changing work environment, is it realistic to expect a job to provide more than just a paycheck?

2. Have you ever had a sense of "calling" in your life? How did you hear that calling?

3. Does God call only a few people?

4. Is it reasonable to expect our work to be part of the fulfillment of our "calling"?

5. Can you tell me what success means for you this year?

6. Are you where you thought you'd be at this stage of your life?

7. Do you go home at night with a sense of meaning, purpose, and accomplishment?

8. If you want different results next year, what are you willing to change in what you are doing now?

Visit www.48Days.com/worksheets for more on Creating a Life Plan.

Chapter 5

Success Is More Than a Job

*Work should, in fact, be thought of as a creative activity
undertaken for the love of the work itself; and that man, made
in God's image, should make things, as God made them, for
the sake of doing well a thing that is well worth doing . . .
Work is the natural exercise and function of man—the crea-
ture who is made in the image of his Creator.*
—Dorothy L. Sayers, *Why Work?*

Pastor Jones sat in my office, slouched down in the big chair,
struggling to relay the events of the last few days. After nineteen
years of faithful service as a pastor, he had been informed that his
contract would not be renewed. No matter how gentle the delivery,
the message screamed out at him—he had been fired. How could
this happen to a man of God? A man who had committed his life
to serving God in the most socially recognized path of service.
The anger and sense of betrayal came exploding out as we began
to explore his options for moving on.

The portrayal of the preceding years, however, relayed a series
of red flags that had been ignored. Pastor Jones was now grossly
overweight, having drowned some of his frustrations in eating.
He was on medication for depression and was being treated for

a bleeding ulcer. Were these not clear signs of a life out of balance? Doesn't God use physical unrest as a method of telling us something is out of alignment? In questioning this gentle, godly man about his current life picture, I discovered his naive theological view. He simply thought that if he were committed to God, somehow everything would just work out. He said he was guilty of "sanctified ignorance." And I've been reminded of that poignant phrase hundreds of times since then in working with people with the same flawed belief.

Sanctified Ignorance

Sanctified ignorance, the belief that if we love God and commit our lives to Him everything will just work out, is an immature theology. If you get up each morning with a clean slate, being open to whatever may happen that day, you will live a life of mediocrity. It is not the path of accomplishment, of excellence, of maximizing our impact and witness. The path of least resistance—just going where it seems easiest to go—creates very crooked streams and very frustrated people. The truly godly life is one of focused purpose, having, like the apostle Paul, defined the goal and created a plan for its accomplishment.

Knowing God's will is not some passive guessing game. Rather it is taking what God has already revealed to us and developing a plan of action. And that revelation comes through our bodies, minds, hearts, and spirits. Yes, we are submissive to God's will, but God is not an angry taskmaster. He will not force you to be miserable day after day. The secret to creating a career that is both nurturing to the soul and the pocketbook is, as theologian Frederick Buechner said, to find where "your deep gladness and the world's deep hunger meet."[1] There you will find a job, a career, a business, and a life worth living. We cannot talk ourselves into doing something we do not inherently enjoy, no matter how spiritual that something may appear to those around us.

Pastor Bob had resented the resistance of his congregation for years. They seemed slow to act and only moderately supportive of his ideas for growth and change. Their resistance was reflected in their lack of financial support. He had two paper routes, requiring him to start each Sunday morning at 3:30 a.m., delivering papers for three hours before delivering his message. His wife was working a stressful job to add to their meager income. And yet all this was justified because he was "serving God." His early interest in engineering had been discarded based on an influential person declaring that Bob was *called* to preach. Even with no affirmation in his work, he was still struggling to fulfill that expectation of another person.

What a dismal picture! Surely God does not call us to this kind of life. *Sanctified ignorance* is no excuse for a life out of alignment, lacking joy, fulfillment, and a clear sense of accomplishment. If you are a street sweeper, then do it with joy. If you are a baker, then do it so that with every new loaf the angels sing. The Bible does not rank the godliness of occupations, however, well-meaning people often do. Look at how God has uniquely gifted you in your skills and abilities, personality traits, and values, dreams, and passions. It is in these that we find the authentic path designed for us to live a life of purpose.

The Wheel of My Life

Each of the categories in the wheel on the following page represents a portion of our lives. Rate yourself by shading in each section the degree to which you are reaching success in that category. (A score of 10 is great, while a score of 1 puts you at the center of the wheel and means you need some work.)

You know what an unbalanced wheel does. It flops and pulls and destroys the overall ride of the car. An unbalanced life does much the same. No one wants to be in the hospital with a heart attack even while having $5 million in the bank. And no one wants to be in great physical shape but have been rejected by family and friends. You cannot justify success in one area at the expense of success in another. Make the decision now to have success in all seven areas, detailed later in this chapter. Learn to recognize when you are making a withdrawal or a deposit physically, spiritually, relationally, etc. Without clearly defined goals in each of these

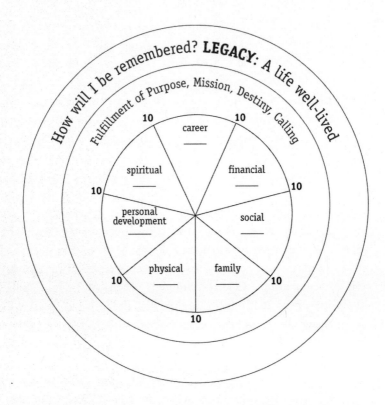

areas, the activities of your life will reflect the desires of those around you.

Need to Pray About It (or Just Indecision)?

Frequently in my life coaching, I notice that people are crippled in life because of indecision. Recently, a gentleman told me that he had been with his company for seventeen years and that he had hated his job for sixteen years and eleven months. My obvious question was, "Why are you still there?" But the fear of having to make a new decision was just too intimidating for him. Consequently, the indecision kept him going to a job he detested.

A common response from spiritual seekers when confronted with any decision is, "I'll need to pray about it." While certainly admirable from a spiritual standpoint, I find this is often nothing but a socially acceptable method of making no decision. Days, weeks, and months go by with unresolved situations and choices. As we all know, it's insanity to continue doing what you've always done and yet expect different results. Continuing indecision and hiding behind a spiritual smokescreen do not lead to different results and higher levels of success. Can you live with the results of your own inaction? Recognize that even making no decision is a decision.

A recent Harvard Business School study asked, "What are the top characteristics of high achievers?" Of course, the list of answers included intelligence, education, and attitude. But at the very top of the list, one characteristic stood out: *speed of implementation*—having the ability to act quickly. The conclusions suggest that eighty percent of decisions should be made immediately.

> *"Man improves himself as he follows his path; if he stands still, waiting to improve before he makes a decision, he'll never move."*
> *—Paulo Coelho*

Jim Rohn spoke to this issue in his book *Facing the Enemies Within*: "Indecision is the thief of opportunity and enterprise. It will steal your chances for a better future. Take a sword to this enemy."[2] In *Think and Grow Rich* Napoleon Hill said, "Indecision is the seedling of fear! . . . Indecision crystallizes into doubt, the two blend and become fear!"[3]

The Bible adds its wisdom in James 1:6–8: "But let him ask in faith without doubting. For the doubter is like the surging sea, driven and tossed by the wind. That person should not expect to receive anything from the Lord. An indecisive man is unstable in all his ways."

Indecision is a crippling characteristic. Indecision in one area will carry its negative effects to other areas of life. I have seen parents who are unsure about selecting a school for their child become almost incapable of functioning for months, agonizing over this

> *"Perfectionism is not as much the desire for excellence as it is the fear of failure couched in procrastination."* —Dan Miller

decision. I have seen frustrated workers who remain in toxic corporate cultures because they are unable to decide to move on. And I have witnessed self-owned businesses slowly fail as the owners feel unable to make the decision to stop their deepening hole.

My wife, Joanne, and I have used a concise process for all the years of our marriage. When confronted with a decision, we allow a two-week maximum for arriving at a decision. Whether it is where to move, what kind of car to purchase, making a career or business decision, or how to handle a difficult relationship with a relative, we approach the process as follows:

1. State the problem.
2. Get the advice and opinions of others.
3. List the alternatives.
4. Choose the best alternative.
5. Act.

And we avoid the crippling power of indecision. Yes, this process must be bathed in prayer. But a daily walk of integrity and character should provide confidence in moving ahead quickly with most any decision.

You, too, can deal effectively with the challenge of making solid decisions. Don't be indecisive and unstable in all your ways. Rather, walk in the strength, confidence, and boldness that come from decisive action.

> *"Indecision and the unwillingness to take action are often described as patience—or 'waiting on God.'"* —Dan Miller

The Power of Having a Goal

Considerable evidence indicates that expectations of your future do, in fact, tend to create your future. It seems reasonable then to spend some time determining specific, worthwhile expectations that will make your life more meaningful. Keep in mind that only about 8 percent of the general population can identify clear goals and only about 3 percent ever actually write those down. These are specific goals, not just the "I want a bigger house and a nicer car" variety. With this process, you can quickly put yourself into the 3 percent category, noting that those 3 percent ultimately accomplish more than the remaining 97 percent.

Remember, in this career and life-planning process you will be identifying your:

1. Skills and Abilities
2. Personality Tendencies
3. Values, Dreams, and Passions

It is in the blending of these three areas that we can create a clear focus and identify work that will give us a sense of meaning, fulfillment—and financial abundance.

The next step after clarifying these three areas is to define goals in the seven areas of life achievement. As goals are identified, the image of the ideal life will emerge. And ultimately, success is *the progressive realization of worthwhile goals.*

 Master Gardener of Your Soul

Our minds are like gardens; they grow whatever we allow to take root.

"Just as a gardener cultivates his plot, keeping it free from weeds, and growing the flowers and fruits, which he requires, so may a man tend the garden of his mind, weeding out all the wrong, useless, and impure thoughts, and cultivating toward perfection the flowers and fruits of right, useful, and pure thoughts. By pursuing this process, a man sooner or later discovers that he is the master gardener of his soul, the director of his life. He also reveals, within himself, the laws of thought, and understands, with ever-increasing accuracy, how the thought-forces and mind-elements operate in the shaping of his character, circumstances, and destiny."[4]

Control your own destiny by controlling what goes into your mind. The books you read, the thoughts you think, the TV you watch, the conversations you participate in, the people you associate with, and the music you listen to combine to create your future. Are you sowing the seeds for the life you want five years from now?

For your purpose in life to be fulfilled, you must set goals in multiple areas. Success is not just career-related or financial; family, physical, and spiritual areas are equally important aspects of achievement. They are part of the same whole. This is the whole-person concept of the *48 Days to the Work You Love* approach.

Time is the only resource you can never recapture. Are you *spending* or *investing* your time? Remember: *A goal is a dream with a time frame on it.*

Personal Checkup: Where Am I Now?

1. Am I missing anything in my life right now that's important to me? ___ YES ___ NO
2. I know what I am passionate about. ___ YES ___ NO
3. I am well organized, know how to focus on my top priorities, and get a lot done every day. ___ YES ___ NO
4. I have a written, strategic plan for my work and personal life with time lines and quantifiable measurements. ___YES ___ NO
5. I have ample time for my family and social relationships and feel good about the balance I have achieved. ___ YES ___ NO

6. I spend time four to five days a week exercising to restore myself physically. ___ YES ___ NO
7. I am regularly achieving my income goals. ___ YES ___ NO
8. My life reflects my spiritual values and I am growing, maturing, and gaining wisdom in this area. ___ YES ___ NO
9. I have studied and developed the new, creative ideas I have had this last year. ___ YES ___ NO
10. I believe I am fulfilling my mission in life. ___ YES ___ NO

 Living My Dreams

Recently in working with a young man, he expressed this sentiment: *"My fear is that I will discover what I love doing but by then be too old to enjoy a full life of living it out."* Wow, what an approach/avoidance conflict. Remember those from your introductory Psychology classes? You want a cookie but know that if you reach for one your hand will get slapped.

What about this above stated fear? When do you cross the line age-wise where it's just better not to want or know about a better life, but better to just exist and wait for the grave? Is it thirty-five, fifty, or seventy? Is ignorance really bliss after all? I've had twenty-seven-year-olds who are fearful that they've missed the window of opportunity for a life well-lived. If your dream was to play quarterback in the Super Bowl, that may be true, but for most of us, living out our dreams is not one event.

Look for recurring themes in things that get your attention. Is it art, music, children, old people, cars, caring and nurturing, birds, reading, flying? Don't think that your dream needs to be new and revolutionary. We all know someone like Susie who sells seashells by the seashore, but most lives of fulfillment may look ordinary to an observer. We find that even those who end up extremely wealthy are not necessarily doing something rare; rather the critical element is that they are doing something they truly enjoy!

Your dream life will integrate your (1) Skills and Abilities, (2) Personality Tendencies, and (3) Values, Dreams, and Passions. Trust your heart in this process. It's more intuition than logic. And be confident you can live out your dreams. Don't settle for less!

Goals

Any stage in life can be an exciting time with many opportunities or a dreary time of confusion and entrapment. You may not be able to change your circumstances, but you can decide that the circumstances won't dominate you. You do have choices.

Something magical happens when you write down your goals. I have seen people transform their levels of success almost instantly simply as a result of getting clearly defined and written goals.

So spend some time determining specific, worthwhile expectations that will make your life more meaningful. If you don't have a written plan for your life, it may feel like you're driving a car without having your hands on the wheel.

On May 6, 1954, Roger Bannister ran the first under-four-minute mile in recorded history. Doctors said it could not be done—that the human heart would explode with such exertion. Six weeks later an Australian runner duplicated that feat. Approximately a year later, eight college runners at a track meet all broke the four-minute mile. What changed? Did humans suddenly evolve to be faster than ever before in history? Not likely. What did happen is that the level of expectation changed. What was believed to be impossible was proven to be possible. Most of us operate under clear beliefs about what we are able to accomplish. If those beliefs are changed, the results change as well.

Zig Ziglar told a famous story about flea training: If you put fleas in a jar with a lid on it, they will desperately pop up against that lid in an attempt to escape for about twenty minutes. Then, while fully convinced they cannot get out of the top of that jar, you can remove the lid. With a perfectly clear path to freedom, those little fleas will starve to death in that jar. They tried escaping once and they *believe* they have no other option. I find many people living their lives within boundaries that exist only in their minds.

Are you a goal setter? Do you typically set goals at the first of the year? If not, why not? Goals give you a starting point and a destination. It is the easiest way to give meaningful direction to your life, which releases you to effectively use your talents.

Identify three-year goals then work backward to what you need to do today to make deposits for where you want to be three years from now. Be specific, creating quantifiable benchmarks to track your deposits of success. Saying you want to be a better mommy, have a better job, or learn a new language is admirable, but without listing steps of measurable, specific goals, you will not move toward any specific action. Then another year will pass without any real change.

> *"The best way to predict your future is to create it."*
> —Stephen Covey

If you can plan out for three years from now, you will likely be amazed at how doors start opening. People who cannot see three years out ultimately end up feeling like victims of circumstances. They feel like they are being pushed along the railroad of life with a locomotive right behind them.

7 Areas for Achievement

1. *Financial:* income and investments (if you can't dream it, it won't happen).

How much do you want to be earning each year in three years? How much do you want to have in the bank or in investments? What are you doing today to move in that direction?

> *"Poverty is not as much a lack of money as it is a lack of choice. But then that lack of choice is often only an illusion—the choice was there all along."*
> —*Dan Miller*

If you can't dream it, it won't happen! Nothing is unrealistic if you have a clear plan.

Don't let failure cripple you. "If thou faint in the day of adversity, thy strength is small" (Prov. 24:10 KJV).

2. *Physical:* health, appearance, and exercise.

Do you take long walks, exercise, or meditate regularly?

Are you living a balanced life? Is this an area that deserves more time?

Can you just give yourself thirty minutes to relax?

Do you know that physical exercise is a cleansing process that can dramatically increase your creativity?

> *"Hearty laughter is a good way to jog internally without having to go outdoors."* —*Norman Cousins*

What are you doing today to maintain or improve your health?

Wealth is difficult to enjoy if you've given up health in the process of getting it.

3. *Personal Development:* knowledge, education, and self-improvement.

Your success, financial and otherwise, will never far exceed your personal development. Start doing something that you've put off because of the risk of failure.

Want to learn a new language? Do it this year.

How many books will you read this year? It is said that if you read three books on any subject, you will be an expert in that topic. Want to know what books I recommend? Send an e-mail to reading@48Days.com and I'll give you my current list of books that can dramatically change your level of success.

Take time for personal development, which is the inhaling part of healthy personal breathing—if you do nothing but exhale, you'll turn blue and pass out. Peter Drucker says, "For knowledge, by it's very definition, makes itself obsolete every few years."[5] The only thing that will allow you to be a leader in today's environment is to be a continuous learner. Don't end your education when you finish high school, college, etc. Why do you think the ceremony is called *commencement?*

Where do you look for inspiration, mentors, and positive input?

What gifts do you have that you have not been using?

Is there some potential for full achievement that needs to be unlocked?

What can you do today to grow in your personal development?

> *"You don't have to burn books to destroy a culture. Just get people to stop reading them."* —Gandhi

4. *Family:* relationship to others, development of children, location of household.

In a speech to graduates of Wellesley College, Barbara Bush said, "Whatever the era, whatever the times, one thing will never change: fathers and mothers, if you have children, they must come first. You must read to your children and you must hug your children and you must love your children. Your success as a family, our success as a society, depends not on what happens in the White House, but on what happens inside your house."

The second law of thermodynamics is things left to themselves tend to deteriorate. Great relationships don't just happen—they come as the result of making deposits toward the "success" you want.

What is the kind and length of vacation you will take this year?

What is your goal for free time with family and friends?

You may try taking the time you normally spend watching a favorite TV show and spend that time instead with your spouse, a child, or a friend.

> *"The best way to make your spouse and children feel secure is not with big deposits in bank accounts, but with little deposits of thoughtfulness and affection in the 'love account.'"* —*Zig Ziglar*

To be a "better" mom, dad, or parent, define what "better" means. You may decide to spend twenty minutes each night with your child or one Saturday morning a month doing what the child wants to do. Or how about scheduling one overnight event with your spouse every quarter of the year?

What can you do today to be more successful in your family?

5. *Spiritual:* seeking, openness, involvement, personal commitment, and Scripture study.

Can you say that you are now living out God's purpose for your life?

What are you a part of that goes beyond yourself?

How have you handled a crisis this last year?

Are you comfortable taking steps of faith, or do you operate with only what has already been proven?

Do you trust your dreams as being inspired?

How will you be remembered?

What will you do today to grow spiritually?

> *"Begin to weave and God will give the thread."*
> —*German proverb*

6. *Social:* increased number of friends, community involvement, etc.

Change old attitudes. Discard past negatives. Ask for forgiveness. Make things right with people whom you need to forgive or who need to forgive you.

Choose someone you could care for or be a mentor to, and then make the effort to work on this relationship starting today.

Spend time with an elderly person and find out some of his fondest memories.

Where do you need to ask for forgiveness?

What is a promise you made to someone but failed to keep?

How do you give encouragement to your friends?

What can you do today to grow socially?

7. *Career*: ambitions, dreams, and hopes.

Your career should be a *reflection* of the life you want; it is an outcome of knowing what you want in the other six areas. Once you decide on the life you want, it becomes obvious what kind of work embraces that. I want to help you plan your work around the life you want.

> *"The greatest good you can do for another is not just to share your riches, but to reveal to him his own."—Benjamin Disraeli*

Don't think there is one predictable path to your ideal career.

Only you have had the experience and "education" that you now possess. That may position you for an opportunity for which few are prepared.

How does your current work contribute to your sense of "mission" and "calling"?

What would your day consist of with ideal work?

What's stopping you from moving toward that now?

What can you do today to start finding—or creating—that kind of work?

These seven areas are integrally connected. They can rise up together or spiral down together. That's why if someone has lost a job, I may recommend that as a first step that person goes for a

> *"If a man does not keep pace with his companions, perhaps it is because he hears a different drummer. Let him step to the music which he hears, however measured or far away."*
> *—Henry David Thoreau*

brisk three-mile walk each morning. Then spend more time with his spouse and play with his children and volunteer in his church and community. Making immediate deposits of "success" in those areas will speed his success in the struggle.

When a person loses a job, we know the first area to be impacted negatively will be *career*. The next immediate one affected is *financial*. With those two in trouble, *family* relationships are likely to be strained, causing *personal development* and self-esteem to crumble. Naturally, he's embarrassed and doesn't want to hang out with the guys right then *(social)*. With all of this negative stress on Monday morning, rather than being out beating the streets, the poor guy is sitting on the couch eating potato chips and watching *Seinfeld* reruns. So *physically* he begins deteriorating—and of course in all of this he wonders, "Why is God angry with me?" *(spiritual)*.

That's not an uncommon scenario. So how can you reverse or prevent that downward cycle? Several years ago I saw a young man who had lost $3.2 million in eighteen months. It was money inherited from his grandmother; unfortunately, he made some bad business investments and lost it all. So career-wise and financially he was in the tank. I had him start going to the Y each morning. This kept his mind occupied, his energy focused and away from the junk food and television. He got in such good shape I think you could probably have bounced quarters off this guy's stomach. I truly believe that the energy and vitality that exploded out of his physical well-being positioned him to very quickly bounce back in the initial areas of lack—which he did.

A few years ago I experienced a major financial disaster myself. I had leveraged one business into the next and was in a vulnerable position when some banking regulations changed. I

"It is good to dream, but it is better to dream and work. Faith is mighty, but action with faith is mightier. Desiring is helpful, but work and desire are invincible." —Thomas R. Gaines

ended up losing everything we had financially. Notice I did not say we crashed and burned or that I failed at everything I did, but I did lose all our money. We lost our custom-built house, our cars, and anything else of value that the IRS could track down. I knew I was a sitting duck for negative thinking to take root and grow quickly.

I borrowed a car from a friend. It was an old, ugly Mercury Zephyr station wagon. The windows didn't work, the radio didn't play, and it used a quart of oil about every one hundred miles. But I carried a little portable audio player with me and started listening to positive material. I listened to everything I could get my hands on that was positive, pure, clean, and inspirational. I was in the car much of the day and I dedicated at least two hours daily to the listening process. I filled all my waking time with positives, leaving little room for the negatives. And I began to experience success in some new areas. I took a job in commissioned sales, experiencing lots of daily rejection but with the quickest income plan I could find.

Those two hours daily had such a profound effect on my thinking and success that I have never discontinued it. I discovered the power of the first hour of the day, what Henry Ward Beecher called "the rudder of the day—the golden hour."

Be very careful how you start your morning. You are planting the seeds for what the day will hold. If you get up late, grab a cup of coffee, fume at the idiots in traffic in your rush to work, and drop down exhausted at your desk at 8:10, you have set the tone for your day. Everything will feel like pressure and your best efforts will be greatly diluted. (In a 2013 study it was observed that 44 percent of wealthy people—income over $160,000—wake up 3+ hours before work while only 3 percent of poor people—income under $30,000—do.)

However, if you get up leisurely after a completely restful night's sleep, you can choose a different beginning. I have not used an alarm clock for the last twenty-five years because I go to bed at a reasonable time and have clearly in my mind when I want to start the next day. I get up, spend thirty minutes in meditative and devotional reading, and then go to my workout area. While spending one hour on the treadmill, I take advantage of my extensive audio library, so that I fill that sixty minutes with physical exertion combined with mental input and expansion. The motivation of Earl Nightingale, Napoleon Hill, Michael Hyatt, Dave Ramsey, and Seth Godin; the timeless wisdom of the TED talks; the theology of Andy Stanley, Deitrich Bonhoeffer, and John Maxwell are the first input into my brain each morning. I never read or listen to the news first thing in the morning, no matter how important it may seem to know. The news is filled with rape, murder, war, and heartache, and that is not the input I want in my brain. Later in the day, I can scan the news for anything related to my areas of interest and quickly sort through what I need. But I carefully protect that first hour of the day, making sure that all input is positive, creative, and inspirational. Many of my most creative ideas have come from this protected time of the day, often when I am in a full sweat. By 9:00 a.m. I am invigorated, motivated, and ready to face anything the day may bring.

 Our Careers Kept Us Apart

I never purchase the sensational magazines in the grocery checkout lane. But I do sometimes glance at the headlines. Recently I saw yet another famous celebrity couple announcing their split with the title, "Our Careers Kept Us Apart." Give me a break! Do they have to do one more movie to make the mortgage payment? One more cover photo to purchase yet another Ferrari? No, this is just an extreme example of misplaced priorities! Here's a quote from the article: "Citing the difficulties inherent in divergent careers which constantly keep them apart, they concluded that an amicable separation seemed best for both of them at this time."[6] Yeah, explain that to the eight- and six-year-old children. "Kids, Mommy and Daddy think having a great career is more important than being a family."

With all the options today, it is critical to define your own priorities. If you simply respond to circumstances, any obstacle will send you in a new direction. Circumstances should not determine our choices. Well-thought-out priorities can guide us through the inevitable changes that will come our way. Careers are tools for successful lives, but nothing more than one piece of a successful life. Without success financially, with family, socially, physically, spiritually and in personal development, career success will be empty and meaningless.

Here are some things Joanne and I have practiced to not only maintain but to thrive in our long-term marriage:

- Treat each other with respect
- Never raise our voices in anger
- Reserve Friday nights for date night
- Do small things just out of consideration for one another
- At least two daily hugs
- Lots of back rubs
- Take a cruise once a year
- Spend time Sunday morning sharing what we're reading

I love my career as an author and coach. But if I had to choose between my current career and Joanne, I would choose her in a nanosecond. I could find plenty of new ways to make an income.

———

From the beginning of this chapter, remember Pastor Jones with his sanctified ignorance? He is redesigning his life as well. The years of moving off track cannot be recaptured completely, but he can redirect to capture the value of his remaining years. He is working in an engineering firm with many opportunities to share his faith and values. His income has increased dramatically, reducing the stress and resentment of his wife and children. He is on a stringent program to reduce his weight and is experiencing the immediate satisfaction of the tiny steps of success. Godly insight and action are replacing his years of *sanctified ignorance.*

Countdown to Work I Love

1. Are you a goal setter? Do you typically set goals at the first of the year? If not, why not?

2. How would you describe your current focus on work?

3. What hobbies do you have? What other skills and interests do you have?

4. How are you involved in your community?

5. What was your father's or mother's attitude toward work and how has that affected you?

Check out www.48Days.com/worksheets for a more complete goal-setting process.

Chapter 6

The Cure for Divine Discontentment

"A Prayer for Joy"

Help me, O God,
To listen to what it is that makes my heart glad
And to follow where it leads.
May joy, not guilt,
Your voice, not the voices of others,
Your will, not my willfulness,
Be the guides that lead me to my vocation.
Help me to unearth the passions of my heart
That lay buried in my youth.
And help me to go over that ground again and again
Until I can hold in my hands,
Hold and treasure,
Your calling on my life.
　　　　　　　—KEN GIRE, *WINDOWS OF THE SOUL*

Ralph Waldo Emerson talked about the concept of "divine discontent," that state of knowing we are not really walking out God's perfect plan for our lives. The popular singing group Sixpence None the Richer has an album titled *Divine Discontent*. It is a musical expression of our justifiable dissatisfaction with things in this life that are causing dissonance or continued unrest. In *Walden*, Henry David Thoreau stated that "the mass of men lead lives of quiet desperation."[1]

When there is a mismatch of who we are and the work we are doing, we experience this "divine discontent." Looking inward at your own uniqueness is a necessary starting point for finding proper career direction. Identifying our inner gifts and talents and using them effectively in our work are critical components of our spiritual wellbeing.

Therefore, looking at job postings or hoping the government or a company will provide a "job" is to reverse the process of finding your own vocation. To look for a job before looking deeply inward is likely to short-circuit the process of finding your calling.

You can structure your work around goals and meaningful relationships and your unique personality, dreams, and passions. Look inward to give shape to the work that is fitting for you, and the application will appear.

Expect change and workplace volatility to enhance your chances of creating meaningful work. It is often in the midst of change and challenges that we find our true direction.

Emerson adds, "A foolish consistency is the hobgoblin of little minds, adored by little statesman and philosophers and divines. With consistency a great soul has simply nothing to do."[2]

 The "Humus" in My Life

If you are a backyard gardener as I am, you appreciate the value of humus—the decayed leaves and vegetable matter that feeds the roots of your new plants. It's interesting to note that the same root word for *humus* gives rise to the word *humility*. This helps me understand that the "humiliating" events of my life, the events that leave "mud in my face" may in fact be the fertilizer in which something new and great can grow.

Several years ago I experienced the business situation none of us wants to face. Handshake relationships with the bank changed and my notes were called. I was forced into selling a health and fitness center at auction, resulting in owing over $100,000 in personal debt. That "humiliating" experience refined my thinking and understanding of business. Today, I am free of bank debt, have a totally nontraditional business, an incredible sense of meaning and purpose in my work, and far more income than I did back in those days.

Remember, it's usually in the midst of muck and mess that the conditions for rebirth are being created.

Looking inward first is the only realistic way to develop a proper direction outward. I tell people that 85 percent of the process of having the confidence of proper direction is to look inward. Fifteen percent is the application—résumé, job search, interviews, etc. Our society teaches us to put the cart before the horse—to get a job and then make your life work. Wrong! To have real "success" you must understand yourself and plan your life first, then plan your work to embrace the life you want. The principles in *48 Days to the Work You Love* are not just a process of rational analysis or a series of tests to define your abilities. Rather, the principles teach a process of learning to pay attention to what God has already revealed to you—people, events, and activities that evoke the strongest response in you. The process is more intuitive than logical, more art than science. Our hearts have to join our heads to find true-life direction. Career testing has always been artificial and inadequate, looking primarily at what you *can* do. Times of change are great opportunities to pay attention to

> *"He who knows others is learned. He who knows himself is wise."* —Lao-Tse

your heart—to see recurring themes in what you enjoy and are
drawn to.

Three Key Areas to Consider

The time spent looking at yourself will provide a 100 percent
payback in terms of helping you create a proper direction. The
more you know about yourself, the more confidence you can have
about choosing the right work environment.

Any job you have must blend the following three personal
areas.

Skills and Abilities

Yes, you must have the ability to do your job, but keep in
mind that skill or ability alone will not necessarily lead to a sense
of purpose and fulfillment. You may have the *ability* to make
perfect wooden wheels, but there may be little redeeming value in
doing so. You may be an excellent dentist and yet be unfulfilled in
doing dentistry. Many people have demonstrated the ability to do
something well and yet are miserable in doing that day after day.
Keep in mind that most career testing focuses on what you have
the *ability* to do. But by the time you reach the age of twenty-five
to thirty, you probably have the ability to do 150 to 200 different
things. Having the ability is not enough reason to spend your time
and energy doing something. It has to go beyond that alone.

Skill areas could include marketing, budgeting, computer programming, serving customers, accounting, supervising, counseling, training, writing, organizing, designing, etc. Pay attention to
those skills that give you pleasure and joy when being used.

Personality Tendencies

This is an area that is often ignored—yet it is often the fatal
flaw in a person's success or failure. How do you relate to other
people? In what kinds of environments are you most comfortable?
Are you a people person, or are you more comfortable with projects
and tasks? Are you expressive and visionary, or are you analytical,
logical, and detailed? Do you like a predictable environment, or do

you seek change, challenge, and variety? Clarification will help you identify the best working situation for yourself.

Unfortunately, success in a position can cause you to be promoted into a position that is not a good fit. The classic book *The Peter Principle*, by Dr. Laurence J. Peter, clarifies how people in our culture are often promoted out of where they function best to a position of incompetence.[3] A bank teller who is loved by her customers may be "rewarded" by being promoted to branch manager where she has to manage the financial details. A great line worker may be promoted to shift boss, turning him into the disciplinarian with the guys who used to be his friends. A great salesman will be promoted to sales manager where he is expected to oversee the scheduling of the staff's work schedule.

Knowing your strongest personality traits should allow you to stay true to those areas that are authentic and enjoyable.

Common personality traits are grouped into four categories:

1. **Dominance (Driver)—Lion—Eagle:** Takes charge, likes power and authority, confident, very direct, bold, determined, competitive.

2. **Influencing (Expressive)—Otter—Peacock:** Good talkers, outgoing, fun-loving, impulsive, creative, energetic, optimistic, variety-seeking, promoter.

3. **Steadiness (Amiable)—Golden Retriever—Dove:** Loyal, good listener, calm, enjoys routine, sympathetic, patient, understanding, reliable, avoids conflict.

4. **Compliance (Analytical)—Beaver—Owl:** Loves detail, very logical, diplomatic, factual, deliberate, controlled, inquisitive, predictable, resistant to change.

You should be able to identify yourself from this list alone. If you'd like a more in-depth report, see my "48 Days Personality Report" at: www.48Days.com/store/personality-profiles.

This is a comprehensive thirty- to thirty-five-page profile, personalized for you alone (and we provide an easy process for your purchase). You'll receive your full report immediately; including a list of suggested careers based on your personal style responses. As a bonus you'll receive a "Biblical Character Match" and have access to my audio Step-by-Step Application Guide. This is the same profile I use as a starting point with all of my personal life-coaching clients, and we have hundreds of churches and businesses that use these reports for team building and accurate job matching.

Values, Dreams, and Passions

What is it that you find naturally enjoyable? If money were not important, what would you spend your time doing? When do you find the time just flying by? What are those recurring themes that keep coming up in your thinking? What did you enjoy as a child but perhaps have been told was unrealistic or impractical to focus on as a career?

This is a tough area for most people. There is a subtle spiritual myth that following our dreams is likely to be selfish, egotistical, and something God would frown on. That kind of thinking implies that God is totally outside of ourselves; we are simply physical robots separated from His mind and heart. However, we are created in God's image and as such are creators ourselves. Why would God have created us to think imaginatively and to have vivid dreams only to then squelch those dreams for practicality? Consider the possibility that your dreams and desires are the voice of your soul, God's voice within you, longing for expression through your faith and action. And as you move toward your values, dreams, and passions, you will move toward being more spiritual and more fully what God created you to be.

We seem to be able to understand if someone has a passion for teaching, medicine, construction, or customer service. Those lead to "real jobs" with real paychecks and benefits. But what if your passions are not so common? Is it possible to follow them anyway? We have seen people develop their passion for art, music, drama, sculpture, growing hostas, wood-carving, baking, and helping the poor into very meaningful and profitable work as well. Don't think that your passion needs to be buried while you do something practical and realistic.

Dreamers of the Day

In *Seven Pillars of Wisdom*, T. E. Lawrence says, "There are dreamers, but not all human beings dream equally. Some are dreamers of the night, who in the dusty recesses of their mind dream and wake in the morning to find it was just vanity. But the Dreamers of the Day are dangerous people because they act their dreams into reality with open eyes."[4]

In today's sophisticated, technological world we often dismiss our dreams as the result of too much pizza or having too much on our minds when we went to bed. Don't underestimate the value of your literal night dreams for problem solving and creative approaches to your situation. And by all means, keep dreaming during the day. Tap into those recurring thoughts and ideas that have followed you for years.

If you can't dream it, it won't likely happen. Success doesn't sneak up on us. It starts as a dream that we combine with a clear plan of action. Become a Dreamer of the Day and watch your success soar.

I find many people have squandered their creative energies by investing largely in the hopes, dreams, plans, and expectations of others. Well-meaning parents, friends, teachers, and pastors may have exerted subtle control to obscure or confuse your own directions. I frequently find professionals in their forties and fifties who are discovering that the life they are living is not their own. Wanting encouragement and support is quite natural, and we seek this first from our nuclear family, then from an ever-widening circle of friends and people of influence. Unfortunately, this encouragement seldom supports a really individualized path, but rather the broad applications of "doctor, dentist, teacher, lawyer, plumber, engineer," etc. Caution is the common response to anything radically different, unique, or creative in application. Thus, after adding the fears

> *"To know what you prefer instead of humbly*
> *saying 'Amen' to what the world tells you you*
> *ought to prefer, is to have kept your soul alive."*
> —*Robert Louis Stevenson*

of friends and family to a person's own, the "safe" path is chosen. And there, caught between exciting dreams and the fear of failure, boring career paths are born.

Thus, the most frequently stated challenge I hear is, "I'm still trying to figure out what I want to be when I grow up." This is often said as an embarrassing self-revelation from a forty-five-year-old, but it is a healthy and realistic starting point. It's very difficult to see all the options clearly and have the necessary self-understanding at eighteen to be able to ask the right questions, much less to be able to make the right choices. Creating proper life direction is an ongoing process—and yes, it can be intimidating and exhilarating at the same time. Value the life experience you have had. Even if unfulfilling and misdirected, it will help provide the clarity by which you can now make really good decisions.

 Your Self-Esteem Is Slipping

If there is one consistent killer of securing a new job or starting a new business, it's the poor self-esteem of the person doing the seeking. Here are some telltale signs your self-esteem may be slipping:

- Poor time management.
- Missing appointments or being late for commitments.
- Slacking off on exercise programs. We take care of what we value and this is a way of saying, "I don't care about myself."
- Dropping out of group involvement. You don't have time this week for school committee, church meetings, study group, etc.

- Becoming a couch potato. The worst time use—combination of what is not urgent and not important. Excessive TV, etc.
- Relationship deterioration.
- Withdrawal from nurturing friendships and personal relationships.
- Low self-esteem is a common initial outcome of job loss.

The cycle is usually one of anger, resentment, unforgiveness, guilt, depression. Depression implies "pressing down energy that wants to be expressed." Depression then leads to more inactivity. Anything that will take you outside of yourself will begin to lessen the cycle. Find a way to be of service and reverse the steps listed above.

Must Everyone Fit the Same Mold?

Frequently, in working on career direction with someone, I realize that person is trying to be in sales when he is skilled in accounting or trying to excel in teaching when she is more gifted in playing music. Why is it that we try to make ourselves something other than what God has designed for us? Part of the pressure is that we rank the value of certain jobs or abilities. Would you rather be an average doctor or an excellent carpenter? Would you rather be a mediocre teacher or an outstanding landscaper? I believe we need to carefully identify the special gifts God has given each of us and then be excellent in the use of those gifts.

Let me use a story to illustrate the pressure many of you feel to perform in ways you may not be equipped for. It begins in school.

Once upon a time, all the animals in a special advanced animal kingdom became very excited about the new school that was being formed for all the animal children. Modern administrators organized the school and adopted a curriculum of activities consisting of running, climbing, swimming, and flying.

All the animal parents flocked to the school, eager to enroll their children in this new progressive school. After all, they wanted the very best for their offspring. Mr. and Mrs. Duck enrolled their son, Davy Duck, and expected great things from him because he was an excellent swimmer. In fact, he was better than the instructor. However, Davy had been in school only one week when the administrators discovered that he was quite poor in running, jumping, and climbing trees. So they made him stay after school and practice those skills. Finally, Davy's webbed feet became so badly worn from climbing trees that he then was only average in swimming. But average was acceptable in this school, so no one worried about this except Davy Duck, who really loved swimming.

Now, Ronnie Rabbit was at the top of the class in running but ended up having a nervous breakdown because of having to do so much extra work in swimming. And Sammy Squirrel was excellent in climbing until he developed cramps from overexertion and got a *C* in climbing and a *D* in running.

Ernie Eagle was a problem child and was frequently disciplined. In the climbing class, he beat all the others to the top of the trees, but he did not follow the procedures for climbing and insisted on getting to the top of the tree using his own method. He was not a good team player and often went off on his own. His teachers could not understand his desire to see new things and reprimanded him for daydreaming in the classroom. Ultimately he was put on Ritalin to try to make him a better student.

At the end of the year, Freddie the goldfish could swim exceedingly well and could also run, climb, and fly a little. Freddie had the highest overall score and was voted valedictorian of the class.

The neighborhood dogs stayed out of school and fought the tax levy because the administration would not add digging and fetching to the curriculum. They had noticed the emotional strain on the other students and were considering starting a school of their own.

How sad that we often diminish our best gifts by struggling valiantly to develop in someone else's area of ability. It is better to focus on your uniqueness and do that with excellence than to end up with mediocrity in several areas. Use this rule of thumb for organizing your work strategy:

- Work where you are the strongest 80 percent of the time.
- Work where you are learning 15 percent of the time.
- Work where you are weak 5 percent of the time.

The fulfilling path is usually discovered right under a person's nose. Normally there are recurring themes in life—moments of recognizing being "connected" or "in the zone." In the great old movie *Chariots of Fire,* Eric Liddle is told by his sister to forget his passion for running and to return to the worthy family missionary ministry. I still get goose bumps when I hear Eric reply, "God made me fast, and when I run I feel His pleasure." Don't ignore your true passions even if the normal applications do not seem to line up with "practical" career paths or produce "realistic" income. A little time spent looking at yourself will provide a big payback in terms of selecting and structuring an opportunity around your unique strengths.

The integration will be critical and will lead you to recognize clear and consistent patterns, identifying areas of opportunity for career application. Look for the unusual application of your uniqueness. If I say "school teacher," the first thing that comes to mind may be a metro school classroom with thirty-two kids in the classroom; however, you could be a teacher working for IBM, living in London, England. All you need is one unique application that integrates your (1) Skills and Abilities, (2) Personality Tendencies, and (3) Values, Dreams, and Passions. This is a very individualized process. There is no cookie-cutter plan for everyone, even if there are similarities in background, age, and education.

> *"Everybody is a genius. But if you judge a fish by its ability to climb a tree, it will live its whole life believing that it is stupid." —Albert Einstein*

Risk—Danger or Opportunity?

I frequently hear someone say they would not want to try a new job, a new sport, a new car, or a different route to the office because of the "risk" involved. Certainly, we hear this especially when a person is considering a new career or changing positions. Why leave the predictable for the unpredictable? And yet, that may be the core of the issue here. If you go to Las Vegas and put the deed to your house down on a roll of the dice, that's gambling—risking with no reasonable control or plan. However, if you are in a negative work environment, you've checked out your options, and are moving to a solid organization with a higher income, how can that be called "risk"? Risk implies jumping off a cliff with no idea what is at the bottom. In business or career moves, we greatly reduce risk by having a careful plan of action. Call it "seizing an opportunity" rather than "risk." Sometimes the greatest risk is not taking one.

Does My Work Have Any Meaning?

Frequently, someone asks me, "Does my work have anything to do with a fulfilling life?" Or "Should I really expect to enjoy my work?"

These questions imply, "Is it just selfish to expect to enjoy my work? Isn't it just part of life to have to work and probably

> *"When written in Chinese, the word 'crisis' is composed of two characters—one represents danger, and the other represents opportunity."*
> —*John F. Kennedy*

not enjoy it?" Many of us grew up with a strong American work ethic—we were expected to work on farms or in factories or other labor-intensive businesses without questioning whether it was something we enjoyed. It was our duty. But look at what has happened by adopting that frame of reference. We began to take less pride in the work we were doing, looking forward only to getting to the weekend.

This attitude about work has undermined our American society. We do the work because we have to. Thus, we are satisfied with shoddy work, treat customers like impositions, and look for excuses to stay home. Consequently, even those who are deeply spiritual have developed a dualistic lifestyle, being spiritual on Sunday—concerned about integrity, character, kindness, and goodness—but then the rest of the week, well, that's just work. This compartmentalization won't fly in any view of spiritual wholeness.

The Bible makes no separation of the different areas of our lives—everything is spiritual. The Bible gives dignity to any work. Any skill God has given you can be used for *ministry*. Jesus was a stone mason/carpenter. Paul worked with leather goods and made tents, and some of the disciples were fishermen. Each of us is called to ministry—and our unique work is our best opportunity for sharing with the world. If we are examples of integrity, character and goodness, we have opportunities all around us for applying our talents and making the world a better place. You really don't need to move to the other side of the world to use your gifts as a form of ministry.

Never separate your work from your worship. See what you do during the week as a form of worship. Remember, you are in full-time service, doing what God has called you to do if you've engaged your unique skills, your personality and your dreams and passions.

 My Boss Is Satan's Offspring

No, I really didn't make that up. As usual, the rich life stories I hear in working with people in transition offer enough real anecdotes that I don't have to be very creative in finding phrases that colorfully describe real situations.

Recently, a very successful young lady wrote this in her pre-coaching form: "My company is going in a strictly money-motivated direction, and my manager may very well be Satan's offspring." She further validated her suspicions with lots of examples that certainly convinced me she was accurate.

How to tell if your boss is Satan's offspring:

- No morality left
- Hatred and fighting
- Jealously and anger
- Constant effort to get the best for only himself
- Complaints and criticisms
- The feeling that everyone else is wrong except those in his own little group
- Envy, drunkenness, wild parties

This list is actually a mixture of this lady's stories and another source I refer to frequently. If it sounds a little familiar, you might want to check the list yourself in Galatians 5:19–23 (*Living Bible*).

Fortunately, we also have a list of what to expect with a godly boss:

- Love
- Joy
- Peace
- Patience
- Kindness
- Goodness
- Faithfulness
- Gentleness
- Self-control

Not too difficult to tell your boss's allegiance, is it?

———

What special abilities do you have? Frequently, I meet with someone to look at career direction and she says, "I can do anything I put my mind to." In essence, she is saying, "Just give me a job." Do you know how unappealing that attitude is to potential employers?

Employers don't want generalists; they want people who know their uniqueness and are looking for opportunities that will allow them to use that uniqueness. No one is impressed by people who are "wandering generalities," or people who haven't really determined their special abilities.

In a job situation you may be able to learn the skills required, but will that alone give you a sense of accomplishment or meaning? No. You can learn to type, knit, shoot arrows, or do brain surgery, but that doesn't necessarily mean you will be happy doing that. What special abilities has God given you? What special desires has He put in your heart? How do you like to relate to people? Do you enjoy lots of people-contact, or are you more task-oriented? Do you like to create, innovate, and go where no one has gone before, or do you prefer to be part of an established team?

These are all legitimate questions, and it is in the blending of all of these that you can find fulfillment in a job. Rest assured, over the long-term no one is really content just getting a paycheck, no matter how substantial that may be. In addition to the paycheck, we all want a sense of meaning, a feeling of accomplishment to what we do. And what we do vocationally is important; the way we spend forty to fifty hours a week is no small matter. Our work must be a fulfillment of our unique ministry; otherwise, we are wasting a lot of our time and energy.

The challenge is to develop a clear focus. If you're just looking for a job, that's what you'll get, just a job. I screen hundreds of résumés for companies, and as soon as I detect that the person will do anything, that résumé goes to the bottom of the pile. It's the person who has a clear sense of how God has gifted her with unique skills, abilities, desires, values, and passions who gets called in for an interview.

Don't be misdirected even if you are presented with something that appears "godly," like going overseas or getting involved with a youth ministry or a home for unwed mothers. If God has not gifted you in the things required there, you will be miserable and so will those around you.

Remember 1 Peter 4:10: "Based on the gift each one has received, use it to serve others, as good managers of the varied grace of God." Be thankful for your uniqueness, and get out there and use it to be excellent, and an example to those around you.

Countdown to Work I Love

1. In what kinds of settings are you most comfortable?

2. How do you respond to management?

3. How would you manage people?

4. Are you better working with people, things, or ideas?

5. Are you more analytical, detailed, and logical, or are you one to see the big picture and respond with emotion and enthusiasm?

6. Are you steady and predictable, or do you seek variety and new challenges?

7. Are you verbal and persuasive, or are you the caring, empathetic listener?

8. What strengths have others noticed in you?

9. In writing your epitaph, what would you want people to remember about you?

Check out www.48Days.com/worksheets to get your personalized Personality Profile.

Chapter 7

Show Me Your Promo Materials

"In the future, most people's jobs will involve scrambling around like frightened chipmunks trying to find the next pay-check in an endless string of unrelated short-term jobs. But since 'Frightened Chipmunk' doesn't look very impressive on a business card, people will call themselves entrepreneurs, consultants, and independent contractors."
—Scott Adams, *The Dilbert Future*

Okay, you must have a résumé. Most anyone you approach in your job search is going to want to see a résumé. And even if they did not ask for it, you need to walk through the process of creating your résumé. I recommend writing and rewriting your résumé if you currently have a job you love, if you already have a job offer for a new position, if you know Uncle Harry is going to ask you to take over the company, or if you want to start your own business. *The process of creating a résumé is one of clarifying your strongest areas of competence. In fact, the process of creating your résumé may be more important than the result of that process.* You will learn how to tell your story.

Don't think that having a perfect résumé is the key to getting your dream job—it's not. At best it's one small tool in the entire process of being offered that dream job. Your personal presentation, responses to interview questions, your work history, your academic background, and your online presence are equally important.

Can I See Your Résumé? I'm Making Paper Airplanes.

Yes, it's almost that bad. A résumé just doesn't have the value it once had. Starbucks attracted 7.6 million job applicants over the past twelve months. Procter & Gamble got over a million applications last year for the two thousand new positions they had. Google hired seven thousand people in a recent year—after receiving over two million résumés. Many companies don't want your résumé. Because of legal issues they are required to keep your application for two years even if they never interviewed you. How do you store two million résumés?

You know what companies do want to see? Your online presence. What will someone see if they do an online search for you? If there's nothing there, you are nonexistent in today's workplace.

Only 19 percent of hiring managers at small companies say they look at the résumés they receive. Union Square Ventures, a New York firm, asks candidates to send links representing their "Web presence," such as 48Days.net, a Twitter account, or Tumblr blog. Todd Carlisle, Google's director of staffing, reads the few résumés he scans—from the bottom up. Google is starting to ask job applicants to fill out an elaborate online survey that explores their attitudes, behavior, personality, and biographical details going back to high school. "Sometimes too much schooling will be a detriment to you in your job," Dr. Carlisle says.[1]

John Fischer, founder and owner of StickerGiant. com, a Hygiene, Colo., company that makes bumper and marketing stickers, says a résumé isn't the best way to determine whether a potential employee will be a good social fit for the company. Instead, his firm uses an online survey to help screen applicants. A current opening for an Adobe Illustrator expert asks applicants about their skills, but also asks questions such as "What is your ideal dream job?" and "What is the best job you've ever had?" Applicants have the option to attach a résumé, but it isn't required.

You can write a blog today and be very searchable instantly. But you have to be consistent about doing something to keep your name and profile easily found. And make sure that's not a photo of you plastered at a Super Bowl party. Recognize that anything on the net is building your professional profile—and will help any company decide if they want you as a team member.

I would suggest this as a minimum:

1. Create a LinkedIn profile.
2. Write a blog (you can do that on 48Days.net without setting up any new template or website).
3. Join two other social networking sites (just find groups that match your interests).
4. Have a Facebook profile (I have only a 48Days profile—not a personal one).

You must decide. What are you doing to make yourself a viable candidate in today's workplace? If you want to be an employee, a consultant, a coach, or business owner—the options are readily available—but you must get in the game or you'll fade into oblivion.

I also encourage you to have an "elevator speech." In the 48 seconds it takes an elevator to go from one floor to the next, you should be able to clearly describe what is unique about you and what you are looking for. The more familiar you are with that speech and the more confident you are that it accurately reflects who you are and what you can offer, the easier it becomes to deliver it with enthusiasm and conviction in a variety of situations.

Here's a quick framework for your elevator speech:

I help _____ ,

do/know/understand _____ ,

so that they can _____ .

It's that easy to define your unique expertise in 48 seconds or less.

Beyond your online presence, a résumé is then an expanded opportunity to present yourself as a candidate for what you want to do next.

However, regardless of your credentials, your eloquence, and your stunning graphics, a résumé is not going to cause people to stop what they are doing and scream, "This is the person I've been looking for!" As I already mentioned, don't get caught up in the fantasy that a "perfect" résumé will get you multiple job offers. A great résumé will get you past the initial screening process and lead to interviews with someone who has the power to hire you. That's all you want it to do.

Getting past this initial screening is not easy, but if you see the whole process, it's certainly possible. Keep in mind that a great résumé provides perhaps 10 percent of the process of an effective job search. In this and the next chapter you will see all the steps in a job search that will help you surpass people with better credentials, experience, and training. Understanding the entire job search process will bring you to offers others will never see.

You do want your résumé to present you as an outstanding candidate for where you want to go. You are not locked into repeating what you have always done. I have helped attorneys, dentists, and pastors redirect their career path by understanding the concept of having "transferable areas of competence."

Building on the Foundation

Writing résumés, searching for jobs, interviewing, and negotiating salaries comprise the logistical part of finding the traditional work you love. Now that you have laid the proper foundation, we can look at these important details. Many people see the résumé as the most important part of the hiring process, believing that companies make hiring decisions from them. A company would be foolish to make a hiring decision from a résumé. You don't want your résumé to tell the company enough to make an intelligent decision about hiring you. All you want it to do is whet the interviewer's appetite so that she wants to see you personally. It is in the interview that the rubber meets the road. Everything else is preliminary.

Your résumé is your sales tool for where you want to go. Don't let it be just a snapshot of where you have been. That may or may not be advantageous for you. Recently, I worked with a gentleman who had managed drugstores for years. In that position, and accurately reflected on his résumé, his primary responsibilities were hiring, training, and supervising employees. Guess what he hated more than anything? Hiring, training, and supervising employees. Why would we present him and position him in a way designed to duplicate those duties? We restructured his résumé to show areas of competence like administration, planning, and operations. These were proven abilities of his and allowed him to present himself as a candidate for something much more behind the scenes with less people contact—aspects far more suited to his personality style.

If you want to redirect your career path, you can begin the process with a well-designed résumé. Remember, if your résumé is just a chronological history of what you've done, it will pigeonhole you into continuing to do what you've always done. You can redirect in major ways by identifying "areas of competence" that would have applications in new companies, industries, and professions.

Make sure your résumé is a sales tool for where you want to go, not just a chronological snapshot of where you have been.

Knowing how to conduct your job search process will transform the results you can expect. Many people become convinced that they are not pretty enough, do not have the right degrees, are too old or too young, or are getting a bad reference from a former employer. How you conduct the job search process will have far more to do with your success than any of those factors.

We are also going to look at how to find the "hidden" job opportunities. We know that only about 12 percent of jobs ever appear in the newspaper, on the Internet, or in other forms of job postings. You can find those unadvertised positions and drastically reduce the competition you face for them.

Even though we know that the average job is now only 2.2 years in length, most people remain unprepared for the interview process. They believe that they can send out their résumé, have some company decide it has to have them, and simply show up for a routine interview. Few things could be further from the truth.

The interview is critical. This is where you sell yourself and negotiate the most desirable position. Time spent in preparation and practice will be a great investment.

Knowing that most hiring decisions are made in the first three to five minutes of an interview confirms that the interviewer is not looking at the fine print on the fourth page of your résumé, but rather is asking herself:

- Do I like this person?
- Will Dan fit in well with the team?
- Is Dan honest?
- Is Dan fun to be around?

These are the questions that are going through the interviewer's mind in those first few critical seconds. Be careful of resting on your academic credentials and work experience. Companies realize that they hire a whole person, not just a set of definable skills. Remember, you are there to *sell* yourself as the best candidate.

Real Predictors of Success

So with all the options and opportunities for jobs, what are the real predictors of success? Isn't *ability* still the best predictor of success?

In *No More Mondays,* I address the five predictors of success:

1. *Passion.* A person with passion is a person who can set goals. Without them, you can have no clear direction and will drift along the road of circumstances.
2. *Determination.* Without a clear purpose, any obstacle will send a person in a new direction. Without determination, you will easily be lured away from your path.
3. *Talent.* No one has talent in every area, but everyone has talent. Discover where you rise to the top. What are those things you love to do whether or not you get paid?
4. *Self-discipline.* Without self-discipline, a person can easily be swayed by others. Self-discipline is the foundation that makes the others work.
5. *Faith.* Even with everything lining up logically, there still comes that step of faith into the unknown. You cannot reach new lands if you keep one foot on the shore.

 Oh I'll Bet You Were . . .

I am increasingly amused while reading current résumés. I know that in today's competitive workplace you need to stand out and I am the first to say that a résumé is a place to brag on and embellish accomplishments. However, we are seeing a blurring of embellishment and downright misrepresentation. The rule of thumb seems to be—exaggerate and confuse.

Rather than reporting being a greeter at Wal-Mart, the new résumé shows "customer service coordinator for Fortune 500 company." The grease monkey at Jiffy Lube becomes a "petroleum distribution specialist." Yesterday's taxi cab driver appears on the résumé as a "transportation logistics manager." The credentials for an eighteen-year-old McDonald's worker become "engineer for meat inspection and preparation." The kid who asked three friends to join Facebook is now a "social media consultant."

Keep in mind that today's "VP of Personnel" was likely a struggling college student herself a few years ago. She probably knows the tricks of the trade, having presented herself as a "human resource specialist" rather than a babysitter.

The bottom line is this: the purpose of a résumé is to help you get an interview. But in today's workplace it plays only one small part in the hiring process—if any. You can bypass the competition with:

- An overview of a major project you've handled
- Photos or examples of your work
- Extraordinary letters of recommendation from people your prospective employer knows well
- A website that showcases your talents
- A blog that is compelling and engaging

If all you have is a great résumé, you may be seen as simply one more person needing a job, whether you are a recent college graduate or a former CEO. *Be prepared to show how you are remarkable, amazing, and spectacular.* Then present yourself with confidence, boldness, and enthusiasm.

Résumé Myths

Consider the following myths and beware:

Myth 1: A Good Résumé and Cover Letter Will Get Me the Job

I wish it were that simple. As I've said before, résumés and letters do not get jobs; they advertise for interviews. A résumé should not tell enough to make a hiring decision. It should simply entice the reader to want to see you. A good résumé will be easy to read and will quickly convey the value of your accomplishments. See it as a sales brochure—like one telling you about a new La-Z-Boy recliner. Did it make you want to go see it and sit in that soft leather, leaning back to let all your stress diminish? That's the same effect you want your résumé to have on the reader. Yes, go ahead and brag on yourself.

- Keep typeface simple. Stay away from fancy fonts and graphics—save that for your wedding invitations.
- Present your information in short, easy-to-read paragraphs. Feel free to use bullet points rather than complete sentences.
- Make sure there are no grammatical errors or misspellings.
- Be specific—state that you increased revenues in your territory from $3 million to $5.3 million in a three-year period or that you reduced office expenses by 13 percent in your first year.
- Don't lie. Be careful about describing yourself as a purchasing manager when you actually picked up the weekly pizza. Don't list yourself as a vice president only because you know that company is no longer in business and there is no way to check on it. And be honest with your credentials. The most lied about item on résumés today is the addition of a nonexistent MBA. Academic degrees are seldom checked and people sometimes fall prey to the temptation to get that extra edge. Don't even think about it. Focus on your areas of competence to make you a top candidate.

Myth 2: The Candidate with the Best Education, Skills, and Experience Will Always Get the Position

Many factors are considered in a hiring decision. Education, skills, age, and ability are only a few of the hiring criteria. Employers interview because they want to see you—how you look, interact, and fit in with their organization.

A recent Yale University study reported that 15 percent of the reason for a person's success is due to technical skill and knowledge, and 85 percent of the reason originates from that person's personal skill: *attitude, enthusiasm, self-discipline, desire, and ambition.*

This is why candidates with the best qualifications on paper frequently do not get the job. We have been sold the myth that a degree is the magic guarantee for fame and fortune. Not in today's workplace. There are plenty of English literature graduates waiting tables and MBAs mowing lawns. Just be realistic about the importance of a degree in your field of interest. Even in high-level positions, your personal characteristics may outweigh the importance of your degrees. Brad Pitt, Russell Simmons, Oprah, Tom Hanks, Michael Dell, Bill Gates, Ted Turner, Maya Angelou, Mark Zuckerberg, Ralph Lauren, and Richard Branson are all college dropouts and yet have achieved high levels of responsibility. (Refer back to chapter 3 for the value of "education.")

Myth 3: Getting a Job Is Really a Matter of Who You Know or Being in the Right Place at the Right Time

Luck is what happens to people who have clear goals and detailed plans of action. Or luck is when preparation meets opportunity. Don't wait on being in the right place at the right time. Create the situation and the circumstances to make you a candidate for the best positions anywhere. You don't have to know the right people—you just have to get yourself in front of the right people. If you do the right things you will be amazed at how lucky you will become. Here in Nashville, Tennessee, I see people who have been waiting for their lucky break in the music industry for twenty-five years. And then I see someone blow into town and two months later is playing in top spots, meeting top label executives, and finding multiple opportunities. It's not luck—it's correct action.

Myth 4: Employers Appreciate Long Résumés Because More Information Saves Time Spent Interviewing

Most résumés get a thirty- to forty-second look. You must be able to communicate clearly in that time your areas of competence. There is no hard and fast rule about having to stay on one page, but there is seldom a reason to go beyond two pages in length. The key is to communicate what has value in positioning you as a top candidate. Include only those things that work in creating the image you want to convey. This is not a historical document but a sales brochure. I have a résumé in my file that is fifteen pages long. The writer has a Ph.D. in chemistry and listed every study she had ever been a part of. Interesting reading but way too much information.

Myth 5: Always Put Your Salary Requirements and History on Your Résumé

This can only work against you. Whether high or low, it has no positive purpose on a résumé. Salary is to be negotiated after the employer decides you are the right person for the job. Only when an employer wants you and you want them is it appropriate to discuss compensation. Anything prior to that will work against you.

Just think about this. If you are applying for a $76,000 position and in your last position you made $41,000, you will be seen as too low a candidate. Similarly, if you made $92,000 in your last position, they may be reluctant to interview you. Keep in mind that compensation packages are very fluid. If you are the candidate they want, the company may easily find another $10,000 to bring you on board. But if you don't get the opportunity to interview, you will miss even having the chance to discuss your benefits to the company.

Myth 6: Always Close a Cover Letter with "I Look Forward to Hearing from You"

Never! Even in times of low unemployment, expecting the receiver to take the initiative is unrealistic. Remember, you must always take the initiative. State when you will call to follow up: "I will call you Thursday morning concerning any questions we both may have and to discuss a personal meeting."

This may appear to be pushy or assertive, and it may be. But what you want is action. Persistence pays. To get the best positions, you will need to stay in the driver's seat in this entire process. No one cares about your success more than you do and no one can present you better than you can. You will need to take the initiative in getting in front of the people who have the ability to hire you. Remember, you have a product to sell and that product is you. The more you approach this process with that mind-set, the quicker and better the results will be.

Myth 7: The More Résumés You Send, the More You Increase Your Chances of Getting a Job

Not necessarily. Thirty to forty résumés combined with quality introduction letters, cover letters, and follow-up phone calls are much more effective than a thousand résumés sent out alone. The Internet makes it so tempting to just send out a million electronic résumés with the push of a button and hope that the law of numbers will work in your favor. That process may be true for playing the lottery, but it is unlikely to work in finding a desirable position for yourself. Well-targeted résumés directed to the right decision makers still get results.

Myth 8: Once You Send Your Résumé, All You Can Do Is Wait

If you take no action, you will likely get no results. Always follow up by phone. Sending résumés without following up is probably a waste of your time.

But just a minute—isn't waiting a spiritual approach to having God open a door? Of course it is. But I see too many people do too much waiting—wringing their hands, sitting at home, waiting for the phone to ring—and too little working in this process. Isaiah 40:31 says, "But they that wait upon the Lord shall renew their strength; they shall mount up with wings as eagles; they shall run, and not be weary; and they shall walk, and not faint" (KJV). There you go—waiting is scriptural. But if we look at the word *wait* in this context we find that it comes from the same word from which we get *waiter*. Thus a more accurate rendering may be to be doing what an effective waiter would be doing—serving and acting based on what they know needs to be done.

"You can do anything if you have enthusiasm. Enthusiasm is the yeast that makes your hopes rise to the stars. Enthusiasm is the spark in your eye, the swing in your gait, the grip of your hand, the irresistible surge of your will and your energy to execute your ideas. Enthusiasts are fighters, they have fortitude, they have staying qualities. Enthusiasm is at the bottom of all progress! With it, there is accomplishment. Without it, there are only alibis." —Henry Ford

Résumé "Objectives" and Other Ways to Waste Your Time

Here is a recent "Objective" on a résumé submitted for my review:

"To support the growth and profitability of an organization that provides challenge, encourages advancement, and rewards achievement with the opportunity to utilize my experience, skills, and proven abilities."

Sounds great—would you like to hire this person? But what do you know about this person? Is she a candidate for flipping hamburgers or for a CEO position? Does he have skills in supervising, organizing, planning, selling, marketing, etc? Is she proficient in any computer skills? We don't know. This "objective" tells us absolutely nothing about the person. It was a total waste of time on the applicant's part. Knowing that most résumés get a thirty to forty second look, you'd better tell the recipient something about yourself that would make them want to see you as a candidate. IMMEDIATELY! Begin your résumé with a skills summary, profile, or expertise. Here's an example of a Skills Summary:

"Over fourteen solid years in technology planning and management. Experienced in strategic systems, organizing and overseeing projects. Knowledgeable in R&D, product development, and financial management. Team player in maintaining company policies and procedures. Expertise with IT businesses, especially those with complex technical, logistical, and implementation challenges."

Don't waste your time with generic lead-ins that get you sent to the bottom of the pile. Use your thirty seconds to convey your "unique value."

Designing a Résumé

Build your résumé so it becomes a sales tool for getting you the position you want. You can present yourself as a top candidate for sales and marketing, administration, organization, developing, training—or whatever your dream position is—if you draw from your experience and identify it in an advantageous way.

Your transferable skills are the most basic unit of whatever career you choose. Once you have mastered a skill in one career, you can transfer that skill to another field and to another career. These skills can also be rearranged, if desired, in a way that opens up a new and different career. Use descriptive terms such as managed, supervised, instructed, planned, organized, trained, directed, edited, recruited, wrote, sold, marketed, created, etc.

The higher your transferable skills, the less competition you face for whatever job you are seeking. Keep in mind that jobs using higher skills are more challenging to find because they are rarely advertised through traditional methods. But the more you understand your areas of competence, the easier it becomes to target those organizations where there could be a potential match.

You always want to claim the highest skills possible. The résumé is the place to brag on yourself; don't be modest. As already mentioned, don't misrepresent yourself, just be bold about how competent you are.

Be specific. If you are reliable, doing what is expected of you and showing up for work on time, you can get any entry-level job today. But as good as they are, those characteristics do little to separate you from everyone else out there. The more specific you can be about what makes you unique, the fewer the competitors and the more you can move up the financial ladder. This may appear to be an irony in a workplace where it appears you must be a jack-of-all-trades. But the reality is that you still need to be able to show unique "areas of competence" to separate yourself from the masses.

There is not one right format for creating a résumé. If you have had increasing levels of responsibility and want to continue in that industry, a straight chronological format may be the best one for you. If you want to redirect your career, then a more functional format will help you. A combination of both chronological and functional is very common and can work well for most people today. The combination résumé is certainly the best choice if you:

- want to change careers and your most recent position has little relationship to what you would really like to do,
- have been a job-hopper with little consistency in the kinds of positions you have had,
- have areas of competence that are part of a position you held several years ago, or
- are reentering the workforce after a lengthy absence.

 Hey, We're Gonna Hire the Weird Guy

In the 1930s, a German psychologist named Hedwig von Restorff documented that things that stand out are more easily remembered. Yeah, that doesn't seem like rocket science information but it does reinforce what we probably already believe. So let's say we read this list to a group and ask them to recall as many items as possible: banana, car, apple, dog, rock, umbrella, fork, Mick Jagger, pen, paper, desk, gravel, tractor, soup.

Okay, it doesn't take a scientist to recognize that you'd probably remember Mick Jagger more easily than dog or rock. In the list, Mick Jagger is atypical and that's why it stands out.

Now think about a hiring situation. A company is doing interviews and has thirty candidates to screen. How does someone end up as a top candidate? Most job seekers are going to have similar GPAs, graduated from similar colleges, and have similar work experience. In a crowded work environment, the candidates that are at the biggest disadvantage are the ones that don't stand out.

I once interviewed for a position where they met with sixty-four guys over the course of two days. I walked into a sea of black suits and realized the immense competition I faced. However, I had worn a pink sport coat. Guess who got hired? Was I the smartest, most qualified candidate? Probably not—but I was hard to forget.

I once worked with an advertising guy who had been fired for some inappropriate behavior at his previous job. But rather than seeing that as a deterrent, he jumped right in the job search, determined to make himself stand out. He sent his résumés out, wrapped in corn husks. Then he did a play on that image in his written material:

- "I'm sure you think this is corny."
- "Ah shucks, just give me a minute of your time."
- "Hey, can you lend me your ear?"

He had immediate and multiple job offers as companies ignored his checkered work history, enticed by the fact that he was remarkable, notable, unforgettable, and weird.

Are you being too careful in your presentation? Are you blending in as just one of many "other guys"?

What could you do to make yourself stand out? Remember, the only thing worse than being remembered for being weird is not being remembered at all.

You should cover at least ten years in your work experience—longer if there is some specific experience that strengthens your presentation. Don't worry if you are just starting into the workforce; draw from areas of competence that you have proven in your school, church, or community. If you have been a housewife for eighteen years, don't present yourself as if you have never had a job. Instead, describe your competencies in planning, budgeting, supervising, coordinating events, fund-raising, promoting, etc. If you are a high school student, describe your abilities in customer service, delivery accuracy, reliability, graphic design, or Internet savvy. Your real experience and competence may make you a stronger candidate than a recently graduated twenty-three-year-old with an MBA.

Having multiple jobs is no longer the red flag it once was. Companies realize that to advance, you may have to move on. They also realize that in today's volatile workplace, good people are frequently let go through no fault of their own. But you don't have to list every position that you held for a very short time. Also, feel free to list only years rather than months on your résumé to draw attention away from the short length of some positions.

 ### Is Job-Hopping Still a Liability?

Changing jobs early and often, or job-hopping, isn't the liability it once was. It might even be a plus. Traditionally, employers who saw a job-hopping pattern on a résumé would pass on that candidate in favor of one with more staying power. But job-hopping isn't necessarily the kiss of death anymore. More and more we find employers actually favoring a candidate who has moved around. Some are even put off by candidates who have stayed too long in one job or one company where their skills, particularly technological skills, have not had to keep pace with the marketplace. In some industries you may have to explain why you stayed around so long. Talk about a reversal in traditional thinking!

———————

One of my podcast listeners shared this: "Dan, I am closing in on age fifty and after thirty-five years in the same position I need to find a new job. I, like others, thought I was in a nice stable position but now we have been purchased by another company and my job is in jeopardy."

I responded: We have to realize—the job is never "stable." Our stability is in knowing what we do extremely well.

Bad References

What if you really don't get along with your current boss? Is leaving out of the question because any new employer will have to talk with Mr. Idiot in checking your references?

Well, for starters, it is very uncommon for a new employer to talk with your past boss. Hiring managers know there are many factors affecting the relationship between employers and employees. Are there others in the company you could ask for a reference? What about that project you worked on last year? Can you use the team leader as a reference? Do you have a former boss who will sing your praises? Do you have customers who will speak well of their relationship with you? How about people you've worked with as a volunteer? Church and community activities are legitimate sources of referrals. Do you have a former professor who believes in you?

And be realistic about the part that references play in your getting that great position. Calling references is usually done after the decision has been made to hire you. No one will waste time calling references unless they have already emotionally decided you are the person for the position. Because of the career coaching I do, I am frequently listed as a reference. I get about three calls a year from prospective employers. With today's job market, few employers even do the checking they should do.

One word of caution: If you are asked about your current boss, be prepared to put a positive spin on what actually occurred. Don't say anything negative about him or her. And don't say anymore than you are asked.

You will find some examples of real résumés in our Worksheets section at www.48Days.com/worksheets. You will see that there are different formats, depending on the purpose of each résumé. Remember, the résumé is only your selling tool in an attempt to get an interview.

Feel free to use as much from the examples as you want. You can copy phrases that apply to your situation, but do personalize your résumé for yourself. Everything in it should work for you. If a piece of information does not help position you as a candidate for what you want to do, don't emphasize or draw attention to it.

Now you are ready to construct or revise your own résumé. Don't make this process more complex than it needs to be. Spend one to two hours and complete it. Yes, it needs to be great, but it's still only 15 percent of the process. Your creative job search, introduction letters, cover letters, phone follow-up, and interviewing skills are equally important components. Create your own look or choose one of the résumé templates found on any word processing system.

Countdown to Work I Love

1. Do you understand your areas of competence?

2. Do you feel trapped because of your current or past work experience?

3. Do you recognize how easily your abilities may transfer to a new industry or profession?

4. Can you see value in those things you may have done as a volunteer through your church or community?

5. Are there skills or training you need to make you a candidate for the work you love?

6. Has God given you abilities that do not match your desires? If so, how can you reconcile those?

Check www.48Days.com/worksheets for Elevator Speech outline and Résumé examples.

Chapter 8

Six Job Offers in Ten Days!

There are two kinds of success. One is the very rare kind that comes to the man who has the power to do what no one else has the power to do. That is genius. But the average man who wins what we call success is not a genius. He is a man who has merely the ordinary qualities that he shares with his fellows, but who has developed those ordinary qualities to a more than ordinary degree.

—THEODORE ROOSEVELT

Yes, I'll tell you about a young man who did get six job offers in ten days—much to his surprise. While he had little to offer in work history, he was prepared in more important ways. Let's go through some basics.

Perhaps you are like many others who are employed but wondering if there is a better opportunity out there. Or maybe you are already "between opportunities" and ready to make the next commitment. Searching in today's work environment is much different from what it was even a few years ago.

Keep in mind the transition we have had from "production work" to "knowledge work." If you show up for work and take your place on an assembly line making lunch pails, you are likely to be involved in production work. When you go home at night, the conveyor belts, the machines, the inventory of parts, and partially completed lunch pails will stay in the company's buildings. Thus, your means of production stays with them.

But if you are in accounting, data processing, sales and marketing, customer service, computer networking, writing, editing, financial analysis, or a host of other similar functions, then at night you take your means of production home with you. Your tools of the trade are largely between your own two ears. Thus your skills are much more transferable than those of production workers. Also, look at how knowledge work improves with age and maturity. If you are laying railroad ties, your ability to perform as a production worker may begin to diminish at about age thirty-five. If you are a knowledge worker, you may continue to increase your options, skills, and marketability well into your seventies or eighties.

Yes, the jobs are changing. Methods of finding new opportunities are changing as well. No longer can you pick up the Sunday paper, see that your local hardware store is hiring, go down on Monday morning, and see your Uncle Fred to get your next job. The volatility, uncertainty, and transportability of knowledge-worker skills have put millions of people into the job search. Knowing that the average job is only 2.2 years in length, even those who are currently employed are looking for the next position. Because of that, the job you see advertised in the paper will also be seen by about three thousand other fully qualified people who may also be viable candidates.

Where Job Leads Come From

So how do we make sense of this situation, and how do we find the best fit? The most effective job-hunting method is this: know your skills, research the potential companies that use those skills, arrange to see the person who has the power to hire you, and request the interview. This method, faithfully followed, leads to a job for eighty-six out of every one hundred job hunters who use it.

In essence, all job-hunting is an attempt for people connections—links between you and the people who make hiring decisions. Gathering information, even about possible job openings, is only the beginning of the process. Many people get mired down in the information-gathering phase and postpone the necessary component of making contact with other people. Getting degrees, certification, or licensure are additional methods of preparation, however, nothing happens until the right people connections are made.

Answering newspaper ads, Craigslist, Monster, HotJobs, and the multitude of other easy-to-find job lists leads to real positions for about eight out of a hundred job seekers. (The higher the level of the job you seek, the less effective this method is.) You need to understand why this is so ineffective.

First, there is a time lag for the job to even appear in any listing. If it is common knowledge that a person is needed, current employees may have already recommended someone who is being hired. It is not uncommon for the hiring decision to have been made before the ad ever appears in any open format.

Second, companies always look for ways to find qualified hires without having to go through the process of screening hundreds of new applicants. So to be run as an ad may indicate that current employees are not recommending the position to those they know (which may say something negative about the open position).

And third, what you see, thousands of others see as well. If it really is a desirable position, they may receive two hundred to three hundred responses, making it very difficult for your résumé to stand out. The odds are against you.

Fourth, many of these ads are blind ads, meaning you can't really tell what the job is or who the company is. Recruiters run these blind ads just to stir up prospects without having real positions available. Many companies run blind ads just to keep a reservoir of candidates. And some companies run blind ads to see if their own employees are looking for new opportunities. If you are spending more than 10 percent of your time using this method, you are wasting time and energy that should be spent in more productive areas.

Private employment agencies and headhunter pursuits lead to jobs for four to twenty-two out of a hundred. No one can present you as well as you can or cares about your situation as much as you do. I get lots of questions about this process. The bottom line is this: you cannot delegate an effective job search. Don't even think about registering with a couple of employment agencies and then sitting at home waiting for the phone to ring. You could still be sitting there six months from now. You must stay in the driver's seat in this entire process. If you use an agency, make that one small part of your overall job search.

Answering ads in trade journals leads to jobs for seven out of a hundred. (Too much time delay, etc.) I have plenty of horror stories about the selection process in these high-level sounding positions. While at her job as a recruiter at a bank, a young lady responded to a nationally promoted position for a university placement director. They had 386 respondents that they narrowed down to eight. She was one of the eight who were then scheduled individually for an all-day interview process, including lunch with the university president and his wife. From that process, they narrowed the field to three. Be aware that this process took place over an eight-month period. My client had already emotionally left her then current position, recognizing her fit for and excitement about this new position. The university then made their selection, not choosing this lady I referenced. I happened to run into one of the committee members soon thereafter and asked how they could possibly have had a candidate superior to my client. He readily agreed that she was by far the best candidate, however, that hiring decision had been made prior to running that original recruiting ad. It was yet one more case of someone's cousin, aunt, best friend's niece, etc., where there was not really an objective selection process in place. They simply went through the motions to satisfy the appearance of equality. My client, reeling from disappointment, quit her current job and went back to her hometown.

Yes, I know the Internet has exploded as a useful tool and is just so appealing as a method of accomplishing everything we need. It is amazingly useful for doing research, getting some additional skills and job search advice. But remember, ultimately you want to get in front of someone who is a decision maker. And unfortunately, most people using the Internet as their primary job search tool are simply hiding out, avoiding real contact, and wasting time. And yes, the ads at Monster.com or HotJobs.com look so perfect to you. Just keep in mind that whatever you see, thousands of other great candidates see as well. While there are exceptions to everything, the results here are pretty dismal. A high percentage of companies who have hired from the Internet report a negative experience. We are seeing a pendulum swing back to what we call "behavioral interviewing," where they really want to see you, talk to you, and eat lunch with you. Plus, recognize that if you are responding to ads on the Internet, you are looking at possibilities all over the world—not exactly the way to embrace personal and family priorities as a significant part of a life plan.

 790,000 Résumés—and You Think Yours Will Be Seen?

Federal rules requiring many companies to keep job applicant data for a year or more are creating hassles for employers inundated with online résumés.

"It's a huge issue for companies, and it's a hot button," says Barbara Murphy, a spokeswoman at Boeing, which received 790,000 résumés last year.

But critics say the rules set up in the 1970s don't work in the Internet age because it's difficult to know the race of faceless online applicants and keeping résumés doesn't make good sense.

Just be aware that the passive system of sending out résumés via e-mail or fax has never worked well as part of a professional job search. It's an easy way to stay busy and not get results.

Better methods for finding a job are available to you.

Applying directly to an employer without doing any homework leads to a job for forty-seven out of a hundred. Just walking in the door, unannounced, works almost half the time. Notice, this is the second most effective method but works best for lower-level positions. If you want a job at Taco Bell, Wal-Mart, Home Depot, or Papa John's, don't waste your time with a fancy job search. Just walk in the door and present yourself as ready to go. I often recommend something similar as part of a transition plan even for professionals. It's not uncommon for a person to be hired on the spot in these kinds of positions.

Asking friends for job leads gets a job for thirty-four out of a hundred who try it. Don't be hesitant about letting others know what you are looking for. In sales, we talk about the "three-foot rule." That means that anytime you get within three feet of someone, you tell them what you are selling. If you're looking for a job, you have a product to sell, and that product is you. So anytime you get within three feet of someone, tell them about that product. It doesn't have to be a whining, help-me-out kind of selling. You can ask for their advice or opinion. Ask what they would do in your situation or how they would recommend finding a match for your skills.

Asking relatives for job leads gets a job for about twenty-seven out of a hundred who use it. Yes, even the family system is not a bad source for finding new opportunities.

Knowing how to do a great job search will serve you repeatedly over the course of your working lifetime.

The old rule of thumb is that the job-hunt process takes thirty days for every $10,000 of compensation. Thus, a $60,000 position will take six months. This is a discouraging statistic, but look at the figures that lead to such a generality. Most people in a job search are contacting four to five companies a month. At this rate of contact, yes, it may take six months. However, finding a position is a sales process and if you understand the numbers involved, you can dramatically increase your rate of success.

If you are selling vacuum cleaners, you may know from the company history that one out of twenty-three contacts will lead to a sale. So then you can decide whether you will make those twenty-three contacts today or if you'll spread them out by only making one contact each of the next twenty-three days. Your rate of making those contacts will determine the timing of your success. Keep in mind that your job search is much the same process. What I lay out here is a short thirty-day burst of focused activity, leading to whatever level of compensation you desire in a much shorter period of time.

Two-thirds of all job hunters spend five hours or less on their job hunt each week, according to the U.S. Census Bureau. If you are serious about seeking a new position, you cannot afford this rate of progress. My advice, based on seeing successful job hunters, is to spend thirty-five hours per week in the search. This will dramatically cut down the time in weeks and months to conduct a successful search.

 ### The Taco Bell Dude

Many of you know my fine culinary habits take me to Taco Bell on a frequent basis. Having vegetarian kids and grandkids makes it a common landing place with something for everyone.

One day I witnessed a job hiring experience that blew my mind. I was sitting there quietly eating my seven-layer (black bean substitution) burrito and saw a young guy (Jeff) walk in with a job application form in his hand. Upon being alerted, the manager came out and sat down with this guy. I was sitting close enough to observe and hear the entire conversation—which lasted approximately four minutes. When the manager walked back to her office I asked the guy—"Did that actually just happen? Did you just walk in the door, meet the manager for the first time, and get a real job offer in four minutes?" He said he had stopped by the day before, picked up an application without talking to the manager, and did in fact just come in for his first interview. He said he had moved to this area two days before and needed something so he could stay here. The manager asked if he could start tomorrow.

After Jeff left I asked to speak to the manager. And I asked her why she hired this guy so quickly. He had a ring in his lip, short pants showing tattoos on his legs and nothing special in his work history. She did not do a background check, a credit history, or call any references. She replied that he was straightforward in his responses, looked her straight in the eye when he talked, and did have a couple previous fast-food jobs. She added that she needed people desperately and would like to add three more people immediately. I asked about the pay level—and she said that while $7.25 is the minimum wage here, she offers her starting employees $8.00/hr.

I've now seen Jeff three or four times. Each time he greets me cordially and I ask him about his job. He cleaned up really well—no more lip ring (which the manager did ask him to not wear) and the long pants hide the racy tattoos. I thought about telling him that if he had cleaned up his presentation first, and with his good personal skills, he probably could have gotten a $15-an-hour job. But he seems happy and I want Taco Bell to stay fully staffed.

The moral of the story is:

- Companies are desperately looking for good people. Granted, this is not a $100,000/year position but it's certainly better than nothing.
- Taking action stills gets results. Up to the $30-40,000 level positions, walking in the door is still a great job search strategy. With a pleasing personality, people are being offered jobs on the spot.
- Sitting at home complaining about the economy or what the White House is doing is not a job

search strategy. Use the Jeff approach, think outside the bun, and start work tomorrow.

Job Search Process

This phase of the process is intensive but short and focused (if you are investing thirty-five hours a week). And don't think that you can't complete this process while you are working. You can. Most people in a job search today are employed. Everything but the interviews themselves can be done without interfering with a normal workday. You simply need to see it as a short burst of intensive energy to lead you to the future you want.

Getting Prepared

Identify thirty to forty target companies. Do you want a place with twenty to eighty-five employees? A profit or nonprofit organization? A manufacturing or service company? A new company or an established one? Do you want to travel or be home every evening? Would you prefer an organization in health, retail, finances, entertaining, or printing? Use the business directory for your city, the Chamber of Commerce directory, an industry guide (readily available at your local library for media, manufacturing, nonprofits, etc.) to help you create this target list. (Most libraries will have both local and national search tools for selecting companies based on your search criteria.)

You are in the driver's seat to choose the companies you would like to work with. You don't have to wait until they advertise a position or you hear someone say they are hiring. Those usual methods typically put you up against seventy to eighty people for most desirable positions, whereas in this method you may have two to three competitors. Remember: when you see an ad for a particular position, you have already lost your best opportunity for that position. Also, this is the method for finding the 87 percent of the jobs that are never advertised. In a rapidly changing workplace, everyone is looking for good people. Be proactive in your search.

Use the three critical steps of the job search:

1. *Send a letter of introduction to each company.* (Send no more than fifteen at a time so you can do the appropriate follow-up.) The letter of introduction is only to build name recognition. Remember, this is a selling process, and we are borrowing here from a sales technique. Let's say a company is selling water treatment systems. If they can get me to see or hear about that product at least three times, my likelihood of buying goes up dramatically. With the introduction letter, we are beginning the same process. You want any potential target company to see or hear about you at least three times. So the introduction letter is the first of at least three contacts in this process.

2. *Send your cover letter and résumé one week after your introduction letter.* Address the cover letter to a specific person. You can get this name from the Business Directory or call the company. Receptionists are wonderful about giving useful information if you ask nicely. Don't bother sending it to the "Personnel Department," "Human Resources," or "To Whom It May Concern." Target a real person who has the ability to make a hiring decision. That will normally be the sales manager, the VP of operations, the president, the office manager, etc. Online search sites like Hoover's online (www.hoovers.com) or www.webopedia.com can give a lot of pertinent information about most companies.

3. *Call to follow up.* This step is very important, but only about one to two percent of job hunters do this. It's very easy to bring your name to the top of the list if you just do a follow-up call. Don't be afraid of being persistent! Call four to five days after sending your résumé. Yes, I know the challenges of screeners and voice mail. But if the process were easy, everyone would do it. You want to stand out. Don't leave messages on voice mail other than to just build in one more opportunity for repetitive name recognition. Don't say anything in this phone message about that person calling you—don't expect it and don't even set the stage for it. If you get voice mail, just hang up and call the receptionist again, saying, "I must have missed Bill. When do you expect him in today?" "What time does he normally get in the office in the morning?"

Gather any information you can. Then when you do connect in a phone call, say, "This is Bill Smith. I'm following up on a recent letter and résumé. I know what your company does and really think I could add to your success. When can we get together and talk?" You'll be surprised how frequently people will say, "Why don't you come by tomorrow at 2:00?"

Keep in mind that if you just send cover letters and résumés, you need to send out 254 to have a statistical chance of getting a job offer. If you combine that with a phone call, the number drops to one out of fifteen—a dramatic difference. Add to that an introduction letter and the results will amaze you. This is a selling process. We use a three-time repetitive process as a marketing principle. Just commit to the process and a time line.

This process, if followed precisely, does get results. In fact, this job search process is probably the key element that has led to the success of the *48 Days to the Work You Love* book and seminar series.

A gentleman who sent out more than a thousand résumés over a fourteen-month period with no job offers was able to get five interviews with three offers (all over $75,000) in a forty-five-day period using this method. Another guy who had gone six months with no interviews received four offers in ten days with this system.

And here's the story about the recent college graduate who received six job offers in a ten-day period using this process. Chuck had a new degree in biology, no relevant work experience, but wanted to get a position as a representative for a pharmaceutical company. He certainly didn't have a stellar sales background, but we capitalized on his great personal presentation skills. He had a firm handshake, a contagious smile, great listening ability, and was sincere about his desire to help people have access to the products that had so profoundly helped his mother in a bout with cancer. He identified the thirty to forty target companies and began his job search exactly as outlined here. Then came the morning of the first interview. He called me immediately after leaving with the great news that they had made him a job offer. I listened carefully, congratulated him, and then told him to turn down the offer. Chuck was flabbergasted that I would suggest such a thing. I explained to him that while the job offer was great, it was not totally in line with what we had targeted—and I assured him that if he continued the job search as he was, there would be other job offers. Although he was thrilled at getting a job offer so quickly and thought his search was over, he reluctantly agreed to do as I suggested. More interviews had already been scheduled, and yes he did receive six job offers in ten days. That's the power of a focused job search.

Remember, no one is going to come looking for you. You must do an active, aggressive search. It's not uncommon for very competent professionals to resist the aggressive nature of an effective job search. They tend to assume that their credentials and great work history will speak for itself and that pushing for contacts and interviews is somehow less than professional. Unfortunately, we are in a marketing environment. It's no longer true that if you "build a better mousetrap, people will beat a path to your door." A clear plan of "selling" is required to find success in any arena. Finding a great job is no exception!

Important note: Again, don't think that I am ignoring the possibilities with the Internet. Yes, I know you can get the e-mails of ten thousand Human Resource directors and have your wonderful résumé in their mailbox this afternoon. However, I also know that 9,999 of them will resent your intrusion. And we know now that 75 percent of the companies that have hired from the Internet have had a bad experience. A concise process of professional contact and persistent follow-up is still the most respected method of contact.

 Unemployed for 18 Months—What Do I Do?

If you've been unemployed for a while, consider your self-esteem.

"People who are unemployed think the worse possible outcome is not finding another job," says Richard Bolles, author of *What Color Is Your Parachute?*

"Actually, the worst part is losing your self-esteem. You start thinking, 'What's wrong with me?'"[1]

Bolles says you must find ways to inject some confidence and optimism into your life because they're essential to a successful job search. He suggests a routine that includes exercise, rest, and plenty of water.

Write down seven experiences at work that you enjoyed and list the skills that you applied in each case. According to Bolles, job hunters typically rely on only one or two methods in their search: mailing out a hundred résumés or posting a copy online. Those might have worked before, but not now.

Don't limit your search to companies that have openings. Consider companies that you'd like to work for, whether they have openings or not. Contact them with the benefits you can bring.

Volunteer or shadow someone on a job you'd like. Get involved in your church and local civic clubs. "You want to take action every day, not sit around waiting for something to happen," says Bolles.

Dealing with Job Search Discouragement

You wouldn't be human if you didn't feel discouragement while you are unemployed. We attach too much of our worth and self-esteem to our jobs, and, consequently, when we are "in-between opportunities," it's natural to feel anxious at times. But you do have daily choices: you can either convince yourself you are looking into an empty future, or you can believe that a better opportunity awaits you. I frequently tell clients that the distance between terror and exhilaration, between hope and hopelessness is often a fine line.

Here are ten tips on how to cope after a job loss:

1. Find selective places to talk honestly about your feelings.
2. Increase your knowledge about the job-search process.
3. Define what you can and cannot control.

4. Live each day fully. Take a fresh look at the success you have in areas other than work.
5. Do something for someone else. Volunteer time to worthy causes or organizations.
6. Build your own support system. Ask for help. Don't hide out in the library all day and never let your neighbors know you are looking.
7. Do something creative. Joanne and I sometimes work on big jigsaw puzzles. You'll find energy for the search if you give yourself creative breaks.
8. Maintain exercise and good nutrition.
9. Maintain hope and optimism. Set achievable daily and weekly goals. Do physical projects where you can see the results immediately.
10. Look for the larger meaning in this transition process.

 Looking Around but Feeling Down

Losing a job can lead to anger, resentment, guilt, and depression. Just recently I was working with a gentleman who, having lost his job, tried to reposition himself and do a job search, only to become discouraged after just a few days with no success. He was hiding out from his wife, pretending to be doing a job search, while in reality he was going to the library to surf the Internet and read magazines. He consoled himself in fast food and high sugar snacks and quickly added about twenty-five pounds. This, in turn, made him self-conscious about his weight and ill-fitting clothes. "I hated my job but am still angry about being let go," he says.

This story is not unusual. New research confirms that losing a job can put people at an elevated risk for emotional and physical problems. Unemployment can start a vicious cycle of depression, loss of personal discipline, and decreased emotional health.

"Depression can contribute to much longer searches," notes John Challenger, CEO of Challenger, Gray, & Christmas.[2]

To break the cycle, take charge of the areas where you can experience immediate success. Increase physical exercise and note the satisfaction of increased vitality and creative thinking. Increase volunteering and feel the rewards of offering a helping hand. Increase positive reading and listening to inspiring audio tapes and find yourself with new ideas. Do special things for loved ones and feel their genuine support and encouragement.

None of these are directly related to getting a new job, and yet they are very much related. From these activities come the boldness, confidence, and enthusiasm necessary to present yourself well.

In this process, remember that everything prior to the interview is preliminary. No one will hire you from a résumé, nor do you want them to. Résumés and the active job search lead to interviews. Interviews get you the job.

Time spent on a good job search is time invested in your future. Don't view it casually. A week spent researching a couple of key companies so that you are more knowledgeable in the interview could mean a difference of thousands of dollars in your income in the next two to three years alone.

Learn how to do this process well; you will have to do it again. *Recognize that you must take responsibility for the success of the process.* No one can do it for you—not the government, the state, the church, or any agency. Be prepared to deal with rejection and then continue being persistent, confident that real success is just a few more contacts away.

You can find examples of the introduction letter, cover letter, and follow-up letter in our Resources at www.48Days.com/worksheets.

Too "Nice" and Too Poor

Here's a recent reader question:

"Dan, I have your *48 Days* book and have started the process of sending out résumés. In your book it suggests calling after a few days to see if they may have questions but a couple of the employers have sent back automated responses saying that they have received my e-mail and that they will contact me but not to call because they won't respond to calls of any type due to volume but to apply again if I don't hear from them in about eight weeks. The question is should I respect their wishes or still try to contact them, as in my original cover letter it says that I will get back with them to see if they have any questions. If I call I could be considered disrespectful, but if I don't then I could be considered someone who lies and doesn't follow through on things."

What a great question! I love the irony of how you either have to be disrespectful or a liar. Fortunately, those are not the only options. Please recognize that most companies discourage contacting them. Just as a homeowner you probably resist having door-to-door salespeople coming around. But if someone really showed up with a solution for the nasty stains in your driveway, you would likely welcome that.

If you think the company is doing you a favor by giving you a job, then by all means, just wait to see if they contact you. BUT—if you think you have something of value to offer them, then use any method to get in front of them to let them know what value you bring.

Years ago I sold advertising to business owners. I highlighted their businesses in a small telephone address book that had their company information on the cover. With no advance notice or appointment I would walk in the door of the business and ask to speak to the owner. I very quickly discovered that people liked what I had to offer them. Sixty-seven percent of the people I talked to wrote me a check on the spot. But probably 85 percent of the office buildings I went into with no advance appointment had signs that said "No Soliciting." Only once in four years did someone criticize me for violating that notice—and in that case I walked across the street and called the angry guy on the phone. I asked him if he'd want his salespeople (auto dealership) to be timid enough to never make a "cold call."

I found that I could give the business owners something they valued and make $4,000 to $5,000 a week in the process. If I had tried not to offend or bend the "rules," they would have missed the opportunity and I would have missed the money.

You have to believe that you have something of value—remember, true "selling" is simply *sharing enthusiasm*. Once you are convinced of the value you offer, break down any barriers to sell yourself. I have coached clients to be waiting in the parking lot for the owner at 6:20 a.m. or to research the address and then walk in the front door of the prospective company. Your clear focus and belief in your value will lead you to boldness, confidence, and enthusiasm.

If you're too nice and too respectful, you'll stay too poor and unemployed.

For many of you, this Job Search Process will be the most important piece of information in this entire book. If you understand and follow this strategy, you can dramatically transform your results, bypassing other applicants with more degrees, credentials, and experience!

Countdown to Work I Love

1. Are some job markets more secure than others?

2. What are the best places to look for new opportunities in today's workplace?

3. What are the biggest mistakes you've made in the past in looking for new positions?

4. How do you feel about "promoting" yourself?

5. How do you know when to change jobs or careers?

6. How should we apply the principles found in Colossians 3:23–24 as workers in this day and time?

Check for current examples of the introduction letter, cover letter, and follow-up letter in our Resources at www.48Days.com/worksheets.

Chapter 9

Do They Like Me?
Do I Like Them?

I learned this, at least, by my experiment: that if one advances confidently in the direction of his dreams, and endeavors to live the life which he has imagined, he will meet with a success unexpected in common hours. He will put some things behind, will pass an invisible boundary; new, universal, and more liberal laws will begin to establish themselves around and within him; or the old laws be expanded, and interpreted in his favor in a more liberal sense, and he will live with the license of a higher order of beings. . . . If you have built castles in the air, your work need not be lost; that is where they should be. Now put the foundations under them.

—HENRY DAVID THOREAU

Most opportunities are secured through the process of an interview, yet many job seekers fail to develop good interviewing skills. Too many people assume the interview is just a formality to follow up the great impression already made with the résumé. But the interview is where the rubber meets the road. And as you probably know by now, this is not a one-time experience. Change is inevitable and "security" no longer exists, so it seems advisable to develop great interviewing skills to deal with these changes as smoothly as possible. Interviewing well is a learned art and should be studied, prepared for, and practiced. Your ability to interview well will translate into job satisfaction and higher income.

Simply stated, a person who does not interview well will not receive an attractive job offer. You may have an exceptional résumé and credentials and qualifications, but if you do not present yourself well in the interview, you will not receive job offers. If you cannot present yourself with confidence and project a professional image in the interview, all your preparation will have been in vain. *You must develop and practice your interviewing skills.*

Remember that in the process of a job search, you are marketing yourself. If you're uncomfortable with selling, you must prepare yourself for this process. You must have knowledge about, belief in, and enthusiasm about the product—and that product is YOU.

Contrary to popular belief, the interview is not designed to be an inquisition or interrogation. The word *interview* is derived from a Latin word that means, "to see about each other." It's important to keep this definition in mind when interviewing. "To see about each other" implies that an interview is a mutual exchange of information. This exchange process not only provides the employer with the opportunity to assess your skills and qualifications, but it also provides you with the opportunity to evaluate the company and proposed position to determine if they match *your* qualifications and needs.

Do not view the interview as a one-sided process. If you are completing a well-planned job search strategy, you will have several interviews leading to two to three job offers. The interview should be an information-gathering process for you as well as the interviewer. The keys to successful interviewing are preparation, knowing what to expect, and practice. Yes, practice is a reasonable ingredient. Most of us do not interview often enough to become proficient at it. Recognizing that interviewing skills translate into satisfaction and income, you would be well advised to practice as you would at improving at golf or tennis.

Preparation, Preparation, Preparation

Preparation is the single most important factor in successful interviews. Your preparation should involve *two primary components: knowing yourself and knowing the company.*

Knowing Yourself

Critical to presenting yourself well and securing a position that will be meaningful and fulfilling is the process of self-assessment. By now you should be intimately familiar with your (1) Skills and Abilities, (2) Personality Tendencies, and (3) Values, Dreams, and Passions. Only by having a clear understanding of these areas will you be prepared to search in a targeted, focused direction. Obtaining a job is your goal; however, be sure that what is required in the position—and the environment connected with it—are a good fit for you, your abilities, and your interests.

Be prepared in this regard to answer the following questions in the interview (more questions will be presented later, but these few are critical in thoroughly knowing yourself):

Tell me a little about yourself. This is a standard question in almost every interview. In some ways, it's probably the most important question in your interview, and you *must* prepare your answer well in advance. The interviewer will expect you to have developed an answer for this question, and if you have not, you will appear ill-prepared, and the interview will be off to a very poor start.

This is your opportunity to sell yourself. Tell the interviewer what you want him to remember about you. You can refer to information you may want to bring up later in the interview. An interviewer can quickly determine if you are knowledgeable and prepared or just another wandering generality hoping to land any job.

Remember, your answer to any question should be no more than *two minutes* in length. On this particular one, you might spend fifteen seconds on your personal background, one minute on your career highlights, a few seconds on your strongest professional achievement, and then conclude by explaining why you are looking for a new opportunity.

Ask yourself, "What can I contribute to this company?" and let that guide your response. Regardless of the content of your answer, you should outline the answer to this question on paper then practice it many times until you can repeat it concisely. Ask a friend or spouse to listen and critique it for you.

What are three of your strengths? If you cannot clearly identify and describe your strengths, how do you expect an interviewer to pull them out in the brief encounter of an interview?

Tell me about a weakness and what you have done to work on it. Don't play ignorant or modestly claim perfection. Be prepared to talk about something you struggle with. At the same time, stay positive in regard to what you have done to improve.

What skills do you possess that have prepared you for this job? Obviously, you need to have researched the company and the job, or you will be unprepared for this question. Again, by now your self-assessment will have made it easy to talk about your unique skill areas and competencies.

What are your short- and long-range goals? Talk about personal goals as well as business goals. Companies today are looking for balanced individuals who are interested in things other than work. Feel free to share these goals. Talk about the opportunity to move up in the company if that is your true desire, but don't say you want to be president.

 Interviewing Flubs

I am continually amazed at what people actually do in interview situations. Every year CareerBuilder.com lists the most unusual things candidates have done in interviews. A recent Top 10 List included:

1. Candidate answered cell phone and asked the interviewer to leave her own office because it was a "private" conversation.

2. Candidate told the interviewer he wouldn't be able to stay with the job long because he thought he might get an inheritance if his uncle died—and his uncle "wasn't looking too good."

3. Candidate asked the interviewer for a ride home after the interview.

4. Candidate smelled his armpits on the way to the interview room.

5. Candidate said she could not provide a writing sample because all of her writing had been for the CIA and it was "classified."

6. Candidate told the interviewer he was fired for beating up his last boss.

7. When applicant was offered food before the interview he declined, saying that he didn't want to line his stomach with grease before going out drinking.

8. A candidate for an accounting position said she was a "people person," not a "numbers person."

9. Candidate flushed the toilet while talking to the interviewer during a phone interview.

10. Candidate took out a hairbrush and brushed her hair mid-interview.[1]

Knowing the Company

Knowledge of the company or organization, its products and services, its standing in the community, and the key individuals involved is essential. In addition, you should obtain information about the company's annual growth rate, annual sales, number of employees, location of the company headquarters, and its major changes such as buyouts or mergers and industry trends. The information you have, which will lead to questions you can ask, can easily tip the scales in your favor during the interview.

The following sources will help you in locating company information:

- Annual reports—available for the asking from any major company
- Business periodicals (*Wall Street Journal, Forbes, Fortune,* etc.)
- Industry magazines
- Dun's Regional Business Directory magazine
- City business directory (available in any major city; lists size, year started, number of employees, contact principals)
- Hoover's Business Directory (get all the business directory information and more; latest stock quotes, quarterly earnings, SEC filings, compensation figures, etc.) at www. hoovers.com
- Moody's Manuals
- Standard & Poor's publications, including Standard & Poor's Register of Directors and Executives
- Thomas Register of manufacturers annual reports (see www.thomasregister.com)
- Better Business Bureau reports
- Chamber of Commerce publications
- Current employees (valuable source for obtaining information)
- Bank of America Small Business Resource Centers (a wonderful resource for in-depth information about any company or organization in the United States)

Most of these reference materials can be found in any major library or on the Internet.

 The 5 Fatal Flaws in Interviewing

Don't assume the interview is only a formality. In fact, it's the beginning of the selling process. Your résumé has gotten you an interview; now you have a chance to actually make them want you for a position. Be careful of committing the following flaws:

1. Lack of enthusiasm: You don't have to be a Jimmy Fallon or a Seth Meyer, but you must express enthusiasm for a job if you don't want to be weeded out immediately. Enthusiasm, boldness, and confidence will often do more for you in an interview than another college degree.

2. *What's in it for me?* We know you want to know about benefits, vacations, etc., but don't lead with these questions. First, the employer will want to know what you can do for them. You can't negotiate for more vacation time before you've been offered a job. Convince the employer that you are the right person for the job, be sure that you want to work there, then you can discuss pay and benefits.

3. *Unclear job goals:* Don't be a generalist. Be clear about the job you are seeking. If the interviewer gets the impression that you are just looking for a job rather than a specific opportunity to use your skills, you will sabotage your chances. You should be able to state without hesitation three characteristics that would make you a great candidate for any given job you are applying for. I am constantly amazed at the people who are looking for "work" without having a clear sense of what the ideal job would be.

4. *Poor personal appearance:* The key here is to fit in with the organization you are contacting. I will defend your right to wear cutoffs and a baseball cap, but if you really want a job, you must dress appropriately. Many times I hear people who are irritated about not being given a job when they have a nose ring, bad breath, and unshined shoes. Keep in mind that organizations hire people, not credentials and experience. If they don't like you, it doesn't matter how great your experience is, you won't get the job. If you're interviewing at IBM, wear a suit. If you're interviewing at Google, wear nice casual clothes.

5. *Not selling yourself:* Even if you would not enjoy selling vacuum cleaners door-to-door, you have to

realize that in the interview process, you are selling yourself. Especially in today's market, you have to promote yourself. Follow up immediately with a thank-you note and a telephone call three or four days later. It's a good way to reinforce your interest in the job as well as ask a question or two you may have forgotten in the interview.

Interview Intricacies

First Impressions

Ten seconds after you've walked into the room, before you even get a chance to sit down, you may have won or lost the job. While you may courteously be given an hour to answer questions and describe your accomplishments, studies indicate the interviewer forms a strong positive or negative impression of you within seconds of greeting you. One university study had job interviewers indicate when they had made a decision by pushing a button on a timer. *Every interviewer pushed the timer within ten seconds.* This lets us know it's not the fine print on the fourth page of your résumé but other factors that take precedence in making the hiring decision.

After that first decision, interviewers tend to gather information to support the decision they have already made. In these first few minutes of an interview, the employer is asking, "Do I like this person? Do I trust this person? Is this person fun to be around?" Although it may be camouflaged, this is where the focus lies more than "Does this person have an MBA in marketing?"

Here are some suggestions to help you create a positive impression:

• The interviewer will schedule the time for the interview and the place where it will be conducted. If you are allowed to choose the time, avoid Monday mornings and Friday afternoons. Choose morning appointments. Research shows that 83 percent of executives are more likely to hire a.m. job seekers. And 70 percent of all hiring decisions are made before 11:00 a.m. So obviously, if you can suggest the time of an interview, make it before 11:00 a.m. Afternoon appointments should be set no later than one hour prior to the close of the normal business day. Again, on Monday, people tend to have too much to do and on Friday they are anticipating the weekend and ready to get out of the office. So the best times for interviews are Tuesday, Wednesday, or Thursday mornings between 8:00 and 10:00.

• Know the exact time and location of the interview.

• Be punctual; arrive five to fifteen minutes early. Don't go in too early, but arrive early enough so you have the opportunity to observe the environment and determine if you would enjoy working there. (Interviewers will be annoyed as much by your arriving very early as by arriving late. Do neither.) To arrive too early indicates over-anxiousness; to arrive late is inconsiderate. The only sensible solution is to arrive at the interview on time but at the location early. That allows you time to visit the rest room and make any necessary adjustments to your comfort and appearance. Take a couple of minutes to relax and prepare mentally.

• Know the name and title of the interviewer. Do not use first names unless asked.

 Is It Me or the "Economy"?

Here's a 48Days Podcast question I received:

"Hi Dan, I am currently applying for a job out of college, and I have had interviews with about ten different companies, but have been turned down in all ten cases. How can I figure out what it is that I do during the interview that makes them turn me down? Is there a way to diagnose this so that I don't keep repeating the same mistake and getting the same result in interviews?" —Sherry

I want to commend you on asking the question as you are. You are asking what you are doing during the interview that makes them turn you down. And that's exactly where you should be looking. If you've had ten interviews we know your résumé is doing its job and people want to know more about you. Something is not working to your advantage in that personal meeting. It's not the economy, not the politicians, not the recession, and not the oppression of the little guy. Look at that person in the mirror and ask the hard questions.

General Rules to Remember

- Smile!! Few things convey pleasantness, enthusiasm, and comfort like a smile. Successful people smile a lot. People who frown are not perceived as happy, productive professionals.
- Be pleasant and outgoing. Do not attempt to take over the interview, but respond easily and spontaneously to questions and the interview process.
- Show self-confidence. Fidgeting, nervousness, glancing down, not accepting compliments, and self-deprecating statements all convey poor self-confidence.
- Do not run down former employers or coworkers. Prepare positive reasons for leaving any former position.
- Show sincere interest in the company and the interviewer. Remember, your task is to "sell" yourself to the interviewer, not to just convince them you are the best candidate for the position.
- Know your résumé thoroughly. Be prepared to elaborate on any part of it. The product you are selling is you—know yourself.

Just as you would promote a product or service, you are now promoting yourself. Effective salespeople know their product, conduct research to determine their customer's needs, and use that knowledge to sell their product. During the interview, the employer or company is the customer and you take on the role of the salesperson. Just as products do not sell themselves, neither do job candidates.

Don't assume the interview is just a formality. In fact, it's the beginning of the selling process. Your résumé got you an interview—now you have a chance to actually make them want you for a position.

The Warm-Up

The interviewer may initiate some small talk about non-controversial matters. Many times the interviewer will find something on your résumé to talk about. Warm-up topics may include weather, sports, or one of your hobbies. The purpose of this warm-up is to help you feel relaxed and to develop a comfortable atmosphere, so you will speak freely and spontaneously about yourself. Remember, however, that from the first instant, you are being evaluated, even if you are not covering issues pertinent to the position.

Question and Answer

The question-and-answer section usually takes up approximately 75 percent of the interview process. The candidate is asked to review her qualifications as presented on the résumé. (Remember that anything presented on the résumé is fair game, so be ready to discuss it. Thus, it's important to have on your résumé *only* items that are sales tools for where you want to go.) After questions about your qualifications and skills, the interviewer will provide you with information about the company. Ideally, you then will be given an opportunity to ask questions. By all means, have four to five questions ready to ask. The questions you ask may create more of an impression than how you answered the previous ones.

QUESTIONS ASKED BY THE INTERVIEWER

The following are some sample interview questions. Write out your answers to these questions; just thinking about them is not sufficient preparation for the actual answering. Writing your answers will help you be more comfortable handling the same or similar questions in the interview. Remember, the interview is not just a formality since the interviewer has seen your great résumé; *the interview is the most important part of the whole process.* Prepare a one- to two-minute response to each question. If you take longer than that, the interviewer may feel you are taking control of the interview.

1. Tell me a little about yourself.
2. What are your greatest strengths? What are three characteristics that would make you a good candidate for this position?
3. What would your previous employer list as your greatest strengths?
4. What motivates you to put forth your greatest effort?
5. What have been some of your most significant accomplishments? How were you able to achieve those accomplishments?
6. What have you done that has contributed to increased sales, profits, and efficiency in positions prior to this one?
7. What types of situations frustrate you? What are your weaknesses? What have you attempted and failed to accomplish?
8. What are you looking for in a new position? Why do you want this job? What do you find attractive about this position?
9. Why are you leaving your current job?
10. What important changes or trends do you see in this industry? How do you think those changes will affect the way we succeed in this company?
11. How long would it take you to make a meaningful contribution to our company? What are the areas in which you would need more training? Do you feel you may be overqualified or too experienced for this position?
12. What do you look for in a supervisor? Describe the relationship that should exist between a supervisor and his employee. What do you see as your most difficult task as a manager? What is your management style?

13. Do you prefer working alone or as part of a team? Are you better working with things, people, or ideas? Are you better at creating or doing?

14. Describe an ideal working environment. In your last position, what were the things you liked most/least? How do you handle pressure and deadlines?

15. What kinds of things outside of work do you enjoy? What magazines do you like to read? Name three books you have read in the last year. Are you achieving personal goals you have set?

16. Where would you like to be five years from now? What would you expect to be earning five years from now? Are you continuing your education? How are you staying current with changes in this industry?

17. How long do you feel a person should stay in the same position?

18. What does a typical weekend consist of for you? What do you do to relieve boredom?

19. What other kinds of positions have you been looking at? If we do not select you for this position, would you be interested in another (office, sales, administrative, etc.) position with this company? How does this job compare with others for which you have interviewed? What makes this job different from your current/last one?

20. Why should we choose you for this position? What can you do for us that someone else cannot do?

21. Do you have any questions? (A good interviewer will ask you this.)

Make sure you are ready with four to five questions. Even if the interviewer has answered everything you need to know, it will make you appear more interested and more knowledgeable if you ask a few questions. Read on for examples.

Want to Nail the Interview? Try This.

In the delightful book *Love Does*, attorney/entre-preneur Bob Goff writes about training his clients who have to give depositions.[2] Other lawyers are firing questions, trying to catch his clients off guard, and he wants them to be relaxed and calm. Here's what he tells them: Have your palms up the whole time. Literally, he tells them to have the backs of their hands on their knees and their palms toward the bottom of the table.

And here's his reason why: "When their palms are up, they have an easier time being calm, honest, and accurate." He says he used to walk around with his fists clenched, defensive and afraid people were going to take advantage of him. But then he says he learned from Jesus to be palms up. "Palms up" means you are strong enough to be vulnerable, even with your enemies. When people have their fists clenched they tend to get angry or defensive—and make mistakes.

Go ahead and try it. Set your hands on your knees and turn your palms skyward. You'll feel an immediate relaxation take over your body. You'll feel more relaxed, less defensive, and ready to deal with whatever is in front of you.

If you're headed to an interview, try this technique. If you have a deadline, spend five minutes in calm breathing with your palms up. If you're making a presentation, have your palms up as you talk to the audience.

Watch the TV pundits, the reality shows, and the other angry guys all around us. Notice how often you see tight fists and clenched teeth. Be careful of trusting those people—being angry and defensive does not align with honesty, kindness, and generosity.

See how many times in the next twenty-four hours you can position your hands palms up. And see your spirit calm, your interactions improve, your relationships soften, and your interviews getting consistent job offers.

———————

UNUSUAL INTERVIEW QUESTIONS

As companies return to interviewing processes that help them understand the whole person, some questions being asked may appear to be a little unusual. The questions may be designed to discover what you value, how you think, or just to see how you respond to a question without a clear answer.

1. What's the biggest career mistake you've made so far?
2. Who else are you interviewing with, and how close are you to accepting an offer?
3. What's the last book you've read?
4. Why do they make manhole covers round?
5. If you had your own company, what would it do?
6. You wake up one morning and there's been a power outage. You know you have twelve black socks and eight blue ones. How many socks do you need to pull out before you've got a match?
7. How many barbers are there in Chicago?

Keep in mind any company is interested in hiring the whole person, not just your technical, administrative, computer, or sales skills.

QUESTIONS TO ASK THE INTERVIEWER

In today's marketplace, it is not enough to competently answer the interviewer's questions. You would be well advised to prepare four to five questions to ask when given the opportunity. *People who ask questions appear brighter, more interested, and more knowledgeable.*

1. What would be a typical day's assignments?

2. What is the typical career path in this position? What is a realistic time frame for advancement?

3. Where are the opportunities for greatest growth within the company?

4. What criteria are used to evaluate and promote employees here?

5. What kind of ongoing professional development programs are available to help me continue to grow?

6. Whom would I report to in this position? What can you tell me about that person's management style?

7. How would you describe the company's culture (personality, environment)?

8. What is the company's mission statement? What are the company's goals?

9. What are the skills and attributes most needed to advance in this company?

10. What has been the growth pattern of this company over the last five years?

11. What do you see as upcoming changes in this industry?

12. Is this a new position, or would I be replacing someone?

13. What qualities are you looking for in the right person for this position?

14. Is there a written job description? May I see it?

15. How many people are in this department?

16. How do you see me complementing the existing group?

17. What do you enjoy about working for this company?

 Smiling for Dummies

An old Chinese saying goes something like this: "A man without a smiling face must not open a shop." I recently ate lunch at a brand new restaurant in Franklin, Tennessee. No one smiled or greeted me when I came in or during my entire visit there. However, there is another established restaurant with the same menu format where I am greeted with enthusiasm every time I visit. Guess where I will go next time.

That same phenomenon has a similar effect on interviewers. In a survey of 5,000 human resource managers, one of the questions was, "What do you look for most in a candidate?" Of the 2,756 who responded, 2,322 ranked *enthusiasm* first. The first thing interviewers look for in a candidate is vitality and enthusiasm. Many candidates with the right background experience and skills disqualify themselves with a demeanor that suggests they lack energy.

The easiest way to convey energy and enthusiasm is to smile. Now there's a tip that you can implement today. No waiting, no paying for expensive degrees, no buying a new suit—just smile.

In the classic little book *The Magic of Thinking Big,* David Schwartz challenges readers with this test: "Try to feel defeated and smile big at the same time. You can't. A big smile gives you confidence. A big smile beats fear, rolls away worry, defeats despondency."[3] That sounds like a great preparation for your next interview.

Exiting the Interview

As you prepare to leave, stand up straight and tall, shake hands, and then pick up your notebook. Make sure the exiting handshake is strong. Practice what you are going to say. Don't be afraid to ask what the next step will be. Have a closing well rehearsed. Ask, "What will be the next step? When can I expect a decision to be made? May I call you on Thursday?" Continue to make eye contact until you turn to exit. Do not ask about salary and benefits at this time. (See next chapter for addressing that.) Summarize your qualifications. Also, state whether you do or do not still want the job. Use this wrap-up as a time to show the interviewer that you have listened and heard what has been said about the company and the position. Make a closing statement that ties in all the information you have obtained from the interview.

Very few people receive offers after a first interview. Therefore, it is very important that you initiate your own follow-up with the interviewer. Your persistence and initiative may be the one small difference in making you the candidate of choice.

Nine out of ten candidates still do not follow up on their interviews. The follow-up letter provides you with a great opportunity to once again put your name at the top of the candidate pool. The thank-you or follow-up letter is to express appreciation for the time of the interviewer and to confirm your interest in the position. It will also help the interviewer remember you clearly and demonstrate your professionalism and writing skills. Remember that with the introduction letter, cover letter and résumé, phone follow-up, interview, and now the follow-up letter, you have created five contact points with the person making the decision. Your name will be hard to forget.

Mention in the letter that you will keep in touch and indicate on what day you will make your first follow-up call. For example, "I will check back with you on Tuesday, August 23, to see if you require any additional information." Mail the follow-up letter no later than the next day following the interview. (You can use e-mail if the interviewer's contact information is offered.)

Continue to make follow-up contacts every four to five days following an interview until a decision has been made. Having invested your time in the interview, you have earned the right to know what decisions have been made. Decisions are frequently made slowly in any organization. Don't be too quick to assume you are not being considered. Your persistent follow-up may ultimately make you the candidate of choice.

Countdown to Work I Love

1. Can you clearly and easily describe your strongest areas of competence?

2. Does knowing that interviewing means "to see about each other" make it more comfortable to ask for information about the company and the position?

3. Are you aware of any personal habits or annoying filler words that may be part of your personal presentation?

4. Is your level of enthusiasm contagious?

5. What are some unusual questions you know of that have been asked of you or others in an interviewing situation? (Incidentally, you only have to pull out three socks to be guaranteed a match. And there's really no accurate way to know how many barbers there are in Chicago. It's just one of those questions designed to see how you approach a difficult task.)

6. How can you be humble and still show confidence?

7. Would you ever take a position even if you knew it was not a good fit for you?

Visit www.48Days.com/worksheets for more interview tips.

Chapter 10

Show Me the Money

*I have learned that success is to be measured not so much by
the position that one has reached in life as by the obstacles
which he has overcome while trying to succeed.*
—BOOKER T. WASHINGTON

The phrase "show me the money" was widely popularized by
the movie *Jerry Maguire*. In the movie, Cuba Gooding Jr. plays a
professional football player and Tom Cruise is his agent. No matter what great position Tom would negotiate for Cuba, the bottom
line was Cuba shouting, *"Show me the money!"* It was a funny and
memorable line in the movie, but how do we approach it in our
own work life?

Is it always self-serving, egotistical, and materialistic to say,
"Show me the money"? Or is it a part of a healthy process we can
learn to do well and in a way that is win-win for everyone involved?
Why is it that people with the same title of "administrative assistant" earn anywhere from $18,000 to $80,000 per year. Some
attorneys charge $40 per hour and some $400 per hour. Is there
really that much difference in ability or training? What is reasonable to expect for the work you do?

> *"A wise man should have money in his head, but not in his heart." —Jonathan Swift (1667–1745)*[1]

How much initiative can you take in this process? Are salaries, bonuses, hourly wages, and benefits written in stone in every company? The answer to that last question is a resounding *no*. Compensation is a very fluid concept and one that can be negotiated in nearly every situation. Finding the right compensation package is still part of the interviewing process.

The first issue to be recognized is that you must totally believe that you are the best person for the position. That comes from being clear on your areas of competence and from having the confidence, enthusiasm, and boldness that can come only from having a clear focus. Then you are ready to present yourself in the most advantageous way. You can't be enthusiastic about a position you don't believe is a good match for you. And you can't be confident about doing something you don't really believe in. The biggest stumbling block for people in negotiating a reasonable compensation is that they don't really want the position or don't really believe they are the absolute best person for the job. In previous chapters we discussed how important it is to make a proper match between the work and what you offer. And yes, now it's time to focus on *the work you love.*

Here's the convoluted thinking of how we often approach work: Work is work. I have to just find a job to pay the bills. If I really did what I love doing, my family would have to live on beans and rice.

Isn't that the typical belief? But guess what? It's not true. Those who move toward the work they love tend to find not only a sense of fulfillment, meaning, and accomplishment, but often find an unexpected abundance in terms of what happens financially. Don't you think it would be easier to be enthusiastic and energetic doing work you love? Don't you think that enthusiasm makes it easier to make more money as well? Of course it does!

In Dr. Thomas Stanley's wonderful book *The Millionaire Mind,* he relates how this issue is lived out by those who are now decamillionaires. Most love their chosen vocations, or, as one of the wealthier members stated, "It is not work; it is a labor of love."[2] Imagine that.

Dr. Stanley also says it's hard for a person to recognize opportunities if he stays in one place and remains in one job—most self-made millionaires have had a rather wide experience with various part-time and temporary jobs. And

> *"I have enough money to last me the rest of my life, unless I buy something."*
> —*Jackie Mason*

finally, if you are creative enough to select the ideal vocation, you win big time. The really brilliant millionaires are those who selected a vocation that they love—one that has few competitors but generates high profits. *If you love, absolutely love, what you are doing, chances are excellent that you will succeed.*

So you've endured the job search process, and now a company wants to have you on board. With the interviewing process coming to an end, it's time to deal with the burning question of compensation. You are thinking, *How much can I get here?* and the employer is thinking, *How much is this person going to cost me?*

Here are some principles to guide you:

Don't discuss salary until:

- you know exactly what the job requires,
- they have decided they want you, and
- you have decided you want them.

The responsibilities of the job determine the salary, not:

- your education,
- your experience,
- your previous salary, or
- your desires, needs, or expenses

To win at the salary negotiation, don't be the first one to bring it up. Instead:

- Show genuine interest in what the job requires.
- Refrain from asking about benefits, vacations, perks, etc., until you know you want the job.
- Say, "Let's talk a little more about the position to see if there's a match," if they ask too early what you need.

Recognize that many things can fall under the title of compensation:

- a company car (How about a new BMW?)
- a country club membership
- free life insurance
- a medical plan
- profit sharing
- company stock
- tuition reimbursement
- additional time off
- relocation expenses
- your own administrative assistant
- a designated parking space
- a sign-on bonus
- weekly massages
- two weeks in the company condo in Hawaii
- your birthday off
- a production bonus upon completion of a project
- educational opportunities for your children
- 401(k) contributions
- a low-interest loan for a home purchase

You get the idea. Make this a fun process. I realize that negotiating anything is not very comfortable for some of you. If you don't enjoy going to Tijuana and bargaining for the turquoise necklace you want, you may be somewhat intimidated by this process. But realize that negotiating salary is not a confrontational process and certainly not a win/lose proposition.

Company Perks—Can I Have Fries with That?

In today's competitive marketplace, companies are getting creative about attracting top talent. A higher salary is just not enough to stand out from all the other options great candidates have today. Ninety-five percent of Americans say they consider a job's perks before deciding to accept an offer. Leading companies overcome the challenge by creating unique benefits and opportunities.

Google offers some pretty sweet benefits. No need for employees to pack a sandwich for lunch or rush home to cook dinner. Free food for lunch and dinner is just one of the many perks here. Employees also enjoy oil changes and car washes, massages and yoga, a play room, back-up child care assistance, and $12,000 in annual tuition reimbursement.

Employees at New York-based Deloitte don't have to just dream about traveling in Europe or volunteering in Africa. The company offers everyone four unpaid weeks off to do whatever they wish, and three to six months of partially paid leave to volunteer or pursue a career-enhancing opportunity.

Employees of Venice, CA-based JibJab Media who make it in to work by 10 a.m. Monday mornings are rewarded with free laundry service. All of the company's employees get a laundry bag to cram as full as possible. What they can fit inside gets washed, folded, and returned the next day.

At Software Advice, employees are encouraged to work remotely from anywhere in the world for a month each year. To date, employees have telecommuted from France, Spain, and Vietnam.

FlexJobs allows its employees to perform under a "Results Only Work Environment" (ROWE). Employees set their own schedules and are not held to any certain number of hours each day. As long as they are accomplishing the goals and are staying "productive and innovative," it doesn't matter when or how they work.

After five years at Ruby Receptionists, employees qualify for the "Five at Five" program—a paid five-week sabbatical. The program provides employees a chance to pursue a dream or activity just for the pure joy of it. In preparation for their sabbatical, employees receive an individual coaching session and a $1,000 grant for their adventure.

At 2HB, a company that provides Systems Engineering and Software Engineering services, employees receive a $50 grooming perk each month. They can use that money for a manicure, pedicure, or just to get a nice hair cut to get that added boost of self-confidence that comes from looking great.

So how does the salary negotiation process actually work? Look at this scenario with me. Let's say Bob goes out to buy a car. He looks at a Toyota Camry and decides that is what he wants. It's a basic model with no extras but seems to be a good buy on a dependable car, to get him back and forth to school. Once he decides on the car here are two possibilities:

1. In the first scenario an inexperienced salesperson breathes a sigh of relief and leads Bob into the Finance and Insurance office before he changes his mind. He will take his little commission and go on to the next buyer.

2. In the second possibility, the mature, experienced salesperson will talk with Bob, asking if he has a favorite kind of music. Of course Bob does. "Wouldn't it be nice to have a great sound system in this car?" the salesman asks. "With spring just around

the corner, you know how much you would enjoy a sunroof. Since you are in school, it will be very important to make this car last for a long time. It would be advisable to have fabric protection, under-coating, and rust-proofing applied. For those long trips back home to family, wouldn't it be nice to have cruise control?" And so on. Ultimately, Bob walks out, a happy customer, but with a purchase price of $1,500 more than he had originally agreed to. Has he been tricked? Of course not. He has simply been shown the benefits of some things he really did want. In the same way, once the company has made its initial decision to hire you, you can freely discuss additional benefits and compensation with little fear of changing the company's basic decision that it wants you!

I recently worked with a young lady who had lost her job, in which she earned over $70,000. Panicked and convinced she could never find another job in that income range, she had decided she would have to start her own business. However, after identifying her unique areas of competence, I advised against that and encour-aged her to do a creative job search. In a short period of time she had two offers on the table; the clearly better fit offered her a base salary of $89,000. We discussed the offer, the fact that it was a great fit, and she went back and asked for $98,000. They settled at a base of $94,000 with some additional benefits, bringing her package to approximately $105,000.

 Here's a Dave Ramsey Listener Testimonial

Dear Dave,

Thank you so much for recommending the book *48 Days to the Work You Love.* I started working for a new company eight months ago and was thrilled to be making my highest salary ever, $96,500. The problem was that I hated going into work every day. I knew that I needed to find different work, but feared that it would be incredibly difficult. The job market in Chicago is still pretty soft, and I wondered whether my chances of finding new employment would be further jeopardized because I hadn't even worked for my current employer for a full year.

I read *48 Days to the Work You Love* and really put its principles into practice. On Day 48, I had a phone interview for a position that I thought I'd love. Exactly one month later, they made me an offer. I start working there on Monday! By the way, I'll be earning $123,000 with four weeks' paid vacation (instead of two weeks at my old job) and my commute will be reduced by 50 percent! Best of all, I'm looking forward to the day-to-day work.

I just loaned a copy of this book to my sister and am talking it up to anyone who will listen. Please keep recommending fabulous books like this one!

Sincerely, Sara McGaughy (full name used by permission)

What are you doing in the salary-negotiating process? Keep in mind that if you have handled the interview as described, salary did not come up until you decided you wanted the job and the hiring manager decided he wanted you. At that point, and not until that point, you are in a position to negotiate. Also, keep in mind that if you have done an effective job search, you should be talking with more than one company anyway. Here is the timing for discussing salary. You discuss salary at the peak.

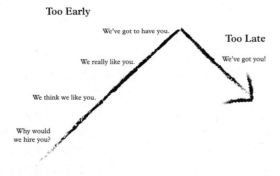

At this point, you should be prepared. You should know what comparable salaries are for the position you are considering. (Check Internet salary sites updated in 48Days.com/worksheets.) That and the responsibilities of the position determine what your compensation should be. A couple of years ago, I worked with a young lady who had been fired from a position in which she made $19,000 per year for clerical work. She decided that wasn't what she wanted to do anyway and began to get focused on what she did want. It was somewhat of a redirection, but she was enthusiastic and confident. After having done an excellent job search, she began interviewing for positions in graphic design and marketing. She interviewed for a position advertised at $32,500. She came out of that interview with a salary package of $54,000. The managers at the new company do not know to this day that in her last job she was making $19,000, nor do they need to know. That has nothing to do with what she is being paid now. She relayed the benefits of what she had to offer and was compensated based on the value of that.

Always focus on the job you are going to, not where you are coming from. There is no law that says your pay will increase by only 4 percent a year or even 10 percent. The world is a very giving place, and if you can convey your benefits, the world will give you what you are worth. Many in the 48 Days community have increased their compensation dramatically because they learned to focus on what they were going *to* rather than looking at what they came *from*.

Also, recognize that your *needs* are *not* the determinant of how you are paid. If you apply at Taco Bell, it is irrelevant whether you have a $1,200 per month house payment and a $450 per month car note; Taco Bell is not going to pay you $40,000 per year to make burritos. Your needs are not the company's concern. Recently, a young lady came into my office in distress. She had spoken to her boss that morning, explaining that she had just moved into a nicer apartment and purchased a new car and could no longer manage on what they were paying her. They fired her on the spot. And I laughed when she told me this story. I totally agreed with the company. What she did to obligate herself to higher payments had nothing to do with how she should be paid.

Have realistic expectations. Many fresh-out-of-college graduates have been asking for salaries on par with people who have twenty years of experience. That's unrealistic because on-the-job experience may be more valuable to the company than the college degree. A far more effective tactic is to ask for a living wage somewhere within the typical pay range along with measurable goals and a commitment to renegotiate the salary if you can exceed all of your six-month or twelve-month goals. Intentionally plan on proving your value and asking for a commensurate raise rather than holding out for an above-average starting salary. That's a fast way to build credibility and get the employer in the habit of thinking highly of you outside of the typical annual review cycle.

Be sure you know your value and then market yourself in that range. In my experience, I find that people often give themselves about a $10,000 window from which to work. If they have been making $60,000, they will look at positions that pay about $55,000 to $65,000. But if they see a perfectly matched position paying $85,000, they don't bother to apply. Be careful of setting your own limitations. You will end up pretty much where you expect to end up.

 Are You on Track to Be Wealthy?

The Massachusetts Institute of Technology has an online "living wage" calculator. For Williamson County, Tennessee, where I live, they say $47,548 is needed for a family of five. This accounts for a telephone, health insurance, and childcare, but does not include restaurant meals, video rentals, Internet access, or vacations. That means someone has to be making $22.86 an hour, or more than one person in the home has to be working. It may come as a surprise to know that 62 percent of American workers do not make $20.00 an hour. Incidentally, the U.S.

Census Bureau shows $23,624 as the official 2013 poverty level for a family of four. The troubling range is between $23,624 and $47,548 where a family is not eligible for government assistance but clearly has difficulty making ends meet.

Wealth isn't made by the hour—it's made with ideas and a plan of action. If you make $15 an hour, you're making $31,000 a year. A cost of living increase of 3 to 4 percent is not going to significantly change your financial position. Yes, you can do a great job and ask for a 10 percent raise each year and in eight years you'll double your income to $62,000. But that's eight years from now. And doubling your pay in an hourly position is not going to happen—unless you bring new skills to the table.

A better question is how can you make an extra $2,600 a month starting now to make that doubling of your income be a reality this next year? What would that do to your debt snowball? Here are some ideas to get your own thinking started:

- Mow 10 yards weekly at $60 each.
- Spend $1,300 on old silver at garage and estate sales; clean it up, know the market, and triple your investment selling it on eBay.
- Create a sports themed sticker package for golf carts and sell 100 at $26 each.
- Buy a fixer-upper in this wild real estate market—do the repairs and make the entire $31,000 in one carefully orchestrated transaction.
- Be the graffiti removal expert in your town. Get ten contracts for $260 monthly to keep a building graffiti free.
- Set up to sell kettle corn at local fairs, festivals, fundraisers, and church events. Book two events a month where you could reasonably expect to net $1,300 each.
- Explore the Fulfillment by Amazon (FBA) program. It allows you to find products, have them featured on

Amazon, and make predictable margins—in whatever volume you can manage.

- Explore the list of my 48 Low-Cost Business Ideas at http://www.48Days.com/48-business-ideas/ to get you started and stimulate your own list.

Nothing here requires another degree or a waiting time. But making an idea work for you does require a break from a paycheck mentality. If you can do that, the sky is the limit in where your income can go—this year.

 Getting Paid What You're Worth

How do you describe what you're worth? Is it based on your age, four times your mortgage payment, your degrees, your years of experience, or your past salary history? None of these matter—get over it. The only criteria for determining your value today is to show your current contribution and level of responsibility.

I've coached lots of people into significantly higher levels of compensation by using the phrase, "Based on the level of responsibility you describe, I would see that in the $_____ to _____ range. Is that still within your budget?"

The biggest mistake people make in negotiating salary is to discuss it too soon. Do whatever you can to avoid talking about salary until you get the job offer. Anything prior to that will work against you.

Keep these principles in mind:

1. *You must make the company money.* As a rule of thumb, you must make the company three to five times your salary for your hiring to be worthwhile. Know the value you can bring to the company. Ideally, have a sense for how hiring you will add to the company productivity and profitability. Then there should be a

way to figure out the approximate business value hiring you will give them. And it's reasonable to ask them to pay you about one third of that amount.

2. *Your compensation always relates to your level of responsibility.* If it's easy to replace you, you aren't worth a whole lot.

3. *Your work is an intangible.* Few salaries are written in concrete. Companies that budget $78,000 for a position will start out trying to hire someone for $65,000. Recognize that the first offer is probably not what the company has in the budget.

4. *Once you agree on a package, get it in writing.* If you've been creative in this process, it's necessary to write out what you verbally agreed on. That way, you don't have to defend later what you thought was said.

Have fun in the process. Don't say yes until everything matches your goals. If you've done a great job search, you should be considering two to three offers.

 ## How to Ask for a Raise

The classic way to ask for a raise seems to be to demand it, or to threaten to quit if you don't get it. Hopefully, it's obvious that this does not work well, as we know that managers tend to give raises to the people they like most. And with unemployment what it is there are probably ten people waiting in line to take your job. So, being liked is a great start to being given a raise. At the same time, your request must be backed up by facts, not just warm fuzzies. Here are some additional tips:

- Ask professional organizations how much someone in your position should be paid. Or check out the standards at www.salary.com.
- Ask for a review. Some companies are notorious for not doing regular evaluations. Don't be afraid to ask for a meeting with your supervisor.

- Be prepared to document your accomplishments. Then you can ask, "Seeing my accomplishments in the last six months, what do you think a fair salary would be?" Don't push to make the boss uncomfortable, but ask, "Can I expect an answer in the next two weeks?"
- Ask for more responsibility when seeking more money. Just being there another year is not a reason to get a raise. More responsibility or productivity is. Ask how you can help your boss or how you can make a larger contribution to the company.
- Be willing to be paid for "results" rather than "time." Being paid for time is an old model and ultimately a destructive business plan. The only thing that keeps you in your job is your contribution to revenue.

Countdown to Work I Love

1. Is negotiating on price uncomfortable for you? Describe three things for which you negotiated the purchase price.

2. Have you negotiated your income in the past?

3. Do you realize that in changing companies you may be able to increase your income by 40 to 50 percent though that is unlikely to happen while moving up in one company?

4. What are the guidelines for how much is reasonable? What is fair? Is it always reasonable to ask for more?

5. Read Matthew 20:1–15. How does this parable fit what you've learned?

6. What would you do if you tripled your current income? What could you offer that would merit that?

7. If your work merited triple your income, would you just live more extravagantly, or what would you do with income beyond your needs?

Visit 48Days.com/worksheets for more negotiating tips.

Chapter 11

Being the Boss You Always Wanted to Have

Examine yourself; discover where your
True chance of greatness lies.
Seize that chance and let no power or
Persuasion deter you from your task.
　　　　—SCHOOLMASTER IN *CHARIOTS OF FIRE*

Wait—what if this whole process of looking for one more job leaves you cold? You still have trouble seeing the right fit in a company and the prospect of once again being vulnerable to the politics of a company doesn't exactly light you up. Maybe it's been a while since you've had to do a job search, or maybe the thought of having a boss half your age is not very appealing. Don't be discouraged! That in itself is part of this process of clarifying what does fit you. And you can choose the work that best fits you—work that fills you with excitement and passion every day. You really can have work that makes you want to get up in the morning; work that says, "This is why I was born!"

Is It Time to Change the Model?

Maybe it's time to be your own boss—yes, to be the boss you always wanted to have. If you are a typical candidate for self-employment, you may never have been clear on what you wanted to do when you grew up. The traditional path may never have been appealing, and the attempt to be a good employee may have always been frustrating. Don't be discouraged! Perhaps you just need a new work model. Even if you thought you knew where you were going, change may have hit you unexpectedly. Downsizings, outsourcings, and management adjustments may have forced you to take a fresh look at where you are and where you are going. Congratulations! Those very factors may have just offered you a new and better option.

Out of the frustration, discouragement, and intimidation, you may recognize excitement and hope just beyond the horizon. You may recognize you have multiple areas of competence and that your years of working for companies have given you training in pretty much every aspect of running the company yourself. This may be your time to tweak the work model, giving you the time control and open-ended income you really want. If you're like many people, losing a job may have been a wake-up call to bring to life that dream that you've been hiding under the carpet since you were a child.

As you work through this process, be encouraged! There is hope! The options today are limitless. You really can be prepared, focused, and ready to move forward with the confidence and enthusiasm that can project you into the next opportunity. I am not suggesting that you jump off a cliff, so to speak, bet the farm, or risk everything. Rather, I am suggesting that this may be a great time to explore all the new models for work that may give you a truer sense of accomplishment, meaning, service, and, ultimately, real security.

> *"The problem with having a job is that it gets in the way of getting rich." —Robert Kiyosaki in* **Rich Dad, Poor Dad**

If you wanted to be an attorney with a large firm, an accountant with a Fortune 500 company, or a physician with a large metropolitan hospital, you would likely have enthusiastic audiences to cheer you on. Parents, teachers, college professors, and friends would encourage, prod, and guide you to success. If you were part of a top sales team or a computer programmer, you would be sent to regular industry seminars and training programs to build your skills and confidence.

But what if you are one of today's growing number of self-employed individuals? Then who cheers you on? Who guides you? Who tells you how to be successful and when to show up for work? Do your former coworkers, bosses, family, and friends encourage you, or do they think you are crazy to want to go out on your own? Do they admire your determination, or do they tell you that what you want to do is not *practical* or *realistic*? When problems arise, will they be sympathetic? After all, you chose to leave the *security, predictability, and stability* of a "real job."

> *"If your dreams do not scare you, they are not big enough."*
> *—Ellen Johnson Sirleaf, the first female elected Head of State in Africa*

In making the leap to being on your own, you may hesitate to discuss your concerns with those you know best. They have their own problems and pressures. Sometimes it's even hard to share your excitement as your success may remind them of their own misery at work. And can they really understand the merit of starting your own lawn maintenance service or dry-cleaning pick-up or senior day care or marketing your own artwork?

Making the shift from a paycheck mentality to making it on your own can be exhilarating and intimidating at the same time. Pushing off from the shore without being able to see the desired port can seem to be a very risky proposition. Yet we know that in today's workplace, staying with a company can also be risky. Just recently I met with a gentleman, who after thirty-two years of faithful service with a major company, was told his services were no longer needed. And at fifty-seven years old, he was not ready or prepared to retire.

Another man at forty-six years old, after seventeen years of rising responsibility with Texas Instruments, was told he had sixty days to find something else to do. Did he think he had *security*? Certainly! But what is *security*? General Douglas MacArthur defined *security* as "one's ability to produce." Your security is determined by your ability to define what it is you do that has value. The clearer you can be on what it is you do well and what provides value for someone else, the more security you have.

Security no longer comes from the company. Many people went to work for company giants like General Motors, AT&T, and Kodak, confident they would put in their appropriate time, and then be taken care of in the retirement years by these grateful companies. Those who went to work for nonprofit, government, or parachurch organizations were even more confident. Surely these organizations would never downsize, layoff, or terminate their faithful servants. And yet we have seen hundreds of thousands from all of these companies, including the IRS, Christian record labels, and publishing companies, being eliminated with no clear solutions for their individual futures. Security has evaporated, as it was historically understood.

Fortunately, technology has reduced the once-staggering cost of starting your own business to sometimes $0. So it doesn't matter that the banker isn't your brother-in-law because you aren't going to need $3 million to buy a bowling alley. Actually, technology has made it easy to run a one- or two-person business from home that even has the appearance of being a big business. I personally have more product sales than many traditional bookstores, yet I have no buildings, no leases, no sign permits, no employees, no worker's compensation, and little day-to-day inventory. Our products are distributed to an international customer base and many of the products we deliver are sent digitally, with no printing, no packaging, and no postage.

Keep in mind the biggest attraction of a self-owned business is not the money; it's the freedom—the chance to control your own destiny. A self-owned business can be the lowest-risk and highest-opportunity option for getting that control of your own destiny. With current technology and the multiple options in the workplace, you can start almost any business part-time and out of your spare bedroom.

 No Money? Start Your Own Business

There is still a popular myth that starting your own business requires a chunk of money. A couple of years ago I noticed there were several tree companies working in our neighborhood. Their assignment was to cut the trees back wherever there was danger of them falling against power lines. Their work often left the trees looking misshapen and distorted, thus the workers were frowned upon and treated badly by most of the neighborhood residents, even though they were doing work that needed to be done. While they were on my property I concluded that I would get better results if I befriended the workers. In doing so I also discovered they had to drive about fifteen miles out in the country to dump each truckload of freshly chipped wood. I asked if they would mind just dumping the chips from my property right there in a big pile. They laughed at the thought of not having to waste an hour driving to their normal dumpsite. What they thought was trash I recognized as a bonus for me.

Over the course of about six months those tree companies brought me approximately 120 truckloads of chips as they cleared branches in my neighborhood. I have used them for nature trails, playground areas, and in covering areas formerly full of rocks and thorns.

And now I have neighbors who have asked me if they could buy chips from me and wondered how I was so "lucky."

If I were looking for another source of income I could sell this "free" product, install playgrounds, or create nature trails as I have done on our property.

Cost of business = zero.

———————

The move from "employee" to a new work model is not the quantum leap it once was. We typically think of someone who leaves a traditional job to do something on his own as an entrepreneur—someone who is driven, aggressive, and not afraid of risk. But the lines are much softer today. People are leaving the cubicles, often with their company's support and blessing, to become freelancers, contingency workers, independent contractors, telecommuters, social entrepreneurs, electronic immigrants, and consultants. Some simply move to being self-employed; some start businesses. Think about the transition from being employed as a bookkeeper to being on your own in the same line of work. As an employee, the bookkeeper has "one client," and in moving away from that model may choose to have eight or ten clients. Not a radical change in work at all. In fact, that move probably allows her to focus more completely on her highest area of competence rather than being expected to fill forty hours a week in a variety of tasks to justify being an "employee." And many times the first client is the company the individual just left as an "employee."

Do You Have What It Takes?

Do you have what it takes to do something on your own—to create work that is purposeful, fulfilling, and profitable? And please dismiss that idea that you must be a hard-driven-in-your-face kind of person to be in "business" for yourself. You may never have a building, employees, or inventory, yet still be a great candidate to move away from the traditional "employee" model.

Over the years, I have identified a number of traits that are strong predictors of a person's success in his or her own business. The more "yes" answers you have to the questions below, the more likely you have what it takes to run your own business. Each of the eighteen questions is followed by a statement of why that particular trait is important.

1. *Are you a self-starter?* Successful business owners are always making things happen. They don't wait around for the phone to ring or to be told what to do next.

2. *Do you get along with different kinds of people?* Every business, even small ones, requires contact with a variety of people: customers, suppliers, bankers, printers, etc.

3. *Do you have a positive outlook?* Optimism and a sense of humor are critical factors for success. You have to view setbacks and small failures as stepping stones to your eventual success.

4. *Are you able to make decisions?* Procrastination is the main obstacle to good decision-making. In a successful business, important decisions are made on a daily basis. Eighty percent of decisions should be made right away.

5. *Are you able to accept responsibility?* If you typically blame others, the company, the government, or your spouse for what goes wrong, you are probably a poor candidate for running your own business. Successful business owners accept responsibility for results even if those results are not favorable.

6. *Do you enjoy competition?* You don't have to be cutthroat, but you must enjoy the thrill of competition. You must have a strong desire to compete, even against your own accomplishments of yesterday.

7. *Do you have willpower and self-discipline?* Self-discipline is the one key characteristic that makes all these others work. Without it you will not succeed.

8. *Do you plan ahead? Every* successful businessperson develops a long-term perspective. Going into business with a detailed plan dramatically increases the likelihood of business success. If you are already a goal-setter, you are more likely to succeed on your own.

9. *Can you take advice from others?* Being in your own business does not mean you have all the answers. Being open to the wisdom and experience of others is the hallmark characteristic of a leader. People who are willing to listen spend more time doing what works the first time, rather than having to experience every mistake.

10. *Are you adaptable to changing conditions?* Change is constant in today's marketplace. In every change there are the seeds of opportunity, thus successful people view change as an opportunity, not as a threat.

11. *Can you stick with it?* Most new ventures do not take off as quickly as we would like. Are you prepared to make at least a one-year commitment to this business no matter how bleak it may look at times? Will you continue even if your friends tell you to throw in the towel?

12. *Do you have a high level of confidence and belief in what you are doing?* This is no time for doubt or second thoughts. You must absolutely believe in what you are doing. If you don't have total belief, you will not be able to sell the idea, product, or service to investors or customers. Don't deceive yourself into thinking that you can do something well you don't really believe in.

13. *Do you enjoy what you are going to do?* Don't ever think you can be successful doing something just for monetary rewards. Ultimately, you must get a sense of meaning and satisfaction from what you are doing. So only consider those ideas about which you are totally passionate.

14. *Can you sell yourself and your ideas?* Many people fail with a great product or service because they can't sell. Nobody will beat a path to your door even if you do have a better mousetrap. Those days are gone. You will need to sell constantly.

15. *Are you prepared to work long hours?* Few businesses are immediately successful. Most require months or years of long hours to get them going. It's like getting a plane off the ground. A great deal of energy is required at first, but once you are in the air, it takes less energy to keep moving. Businesses are very much the same.

16. *Do you have the physical and emotional energy to run a business?* Operating your own business can be more draining than

working for someone else because you have to make all the decisions and probably do all the work (initially, at least).

17. *Do you have the support of your family and/or spouse?* Without support at home, your chances of success are dramatically reduced. Doubt and misgivings can creep in too easily.

18. *Are you willing to risk your own money in this venture?* If you're not, you probably question your confidence in the venture and your commitment to it. No bank or outside lender will be willing to take a risk if you are not willing to back it with everything you have.

More and more people are looking for greater control of their destinies and for the freedom that having their own business allows. Make sure you match your personal skills with the proper business choice. Your work must integrate your skills, your personality tendencies, and your interests. That may seem simple and obvious, but it is amazing how often those principles are violated. The more you know and understand about yourself and match that up with your business direction, the more you exponentially increase your chances for success.

Are You a Candidate?

If you think and make decisions like an employee, being on your own becomes an agonizing experience. Customers don't buy when they've indicated they will, equipment breaks when you least expect it, workers don't show up as planned, and the landlord raises the rent unexpectedly. In many ways, the characteristics that make a person a good employee are often the exact opposite of those that make a successful self-employed individual. Being loyal, predictable, and doing what others expect may, in fact, sabotage your best entrepreneurial efforts.

Many of the standard business methods may not apply to what you are trying to do. Jack Dorsey (Twitter), Sara Blakely (SPANX), Blake Mycoskie (TOMS), and Mark Zuckerberg (Facebook) did not follow standard business methods in building their companies. And for your business, workers compensation, lease agreements, and complicated accounting practices may have little relevance. Traditional knowledge of business plans and principles may not address the needs of today's freelancers, home-based business people, craftsmen, artists, writers, consultants, and contract workers whose numbers are exploding.

Even the traditional predictors (intelligence and education) may not provide much correlation to success for the self-employed person. In his popular book *Emotional Intelligence*, Daniel Goleman states, "There are widespread exceptions to the rule that IQ predicts success—there are more exceptions than cases that fit the rule. At best, IQ contributes about 20 percent to the factors that determine life success, which leaves 80 percent to other forces."[1] He goes on to describe these *other forces* as "emotional intelligence": "abilities such as being able to motivate [yourself] and persist in the face of frustrations; to control impulse and delay gratification; to regulate [your] moods and keep distress from swamping the ability to think; to empathize and hope." These other forces—the 80 percent determinants of success—also include attitude, enthusiasm, energy, and tone of voice.

Richard Branson, the flamboyant billionaire founder of the Virgin empire (which encompasses more than four hundred businesses), was a dyslexic, academically struggling kid who did poorly on any IQ test. However, at age seventeen, while still in boarding school, Branson published an innovative newspaper called *Student*. He solicited corporate advertisers, linked students across schools, and filled the paper with articles written by rock stars, movie celebrities, and ministers of British Parliament. It was a huge business and financial success. The headmaster of his boarding school summed it up like this: "Congratulations, Branson. I predict that you will either go to prison or become a millionaire." Not a bad way for a guy who couldn't read well.

The downsizing of corporate America and the accompanying insecurity have fueled a resurgence of nontraditional work. These factors have also prompted the concept of having a core career, in which a person has a job that keeps a roof overhead and food on the table but also has one or two other profit-producing ideas in place as well. With the exploding opportunities in home-based

> *Two men were walking along a crowded sidewalk*
> *in a downtown business area. Suddenly one*
> *exclaimed: "Listen to the lovely sound of that*
> *cricket." But the other could not hear. He asked*
> *his companion how he could detect the sound of a*
> *cricket amid the din of people and traffic. The first*
> *man, who was a zoologist, had trained himself*
> *to listen to the voices of nature. But he didn't*
> *explain. He simply took a coin out of his pocket*
> *and dropped it to the sidewalk, whereupon a*
> *dozen people began to look about them.*
> *"We hear," he said, "what we listen for."*
> —**Kermit L. Long, taken from The Three**
> **Boxes of Life by Richard Bolles**

businesses, many people are finding that it makes more sense to use this model than to attempt to find the one right job that provides all their needs. One of the hottest terms for creating a work life today is "multiple streams of income." You may have two or three things that are creating income for you, rather than only one all-important job.

I happen to have seven areas of income; all with no employees and none with the look of a traditional business. I coach people individually, sell books and computerized profiles, have facilitators around the country teaching the *48 Days* material, write articles for magazines and websites, coordinate a Mastermind group, host live events on finding your purpose, speak at conferences, promote affiliate connections, produce a weekly on-demand radio show, etc.

You may not see yourself as a typical entrepreneur or business owner. But in going through any transition you must recognize all the options for selecting work. It would be shortsighted to look for only a traditional job when that model is diminishing. Just be aware of the new work models and ways to apply your unique skills.

Currently, about 60 percent of American homes have a business operating within their walls. One in four (22 percent) businesses with employees operate out of someone's home. The median space occupied by the business is about 250 square feet, the size of a bedroom in a middle-class home. It also does not mean that this is just someone selling a little soap or makeup and bringing in an extra $100 a month. A recent IDC Survey (IDC, a subsidiary of International Data Group) indicates that the average income for income-generating home offices is $63,000 a year. According to *Money* magazine, 20 percent have yearly incomes of $100,000 to $500,000. Today women run 70 percent of those home-based businesses. Research shows that as traditional unemployment has spiraled up, home-based businesses are creating an estimated eight-five hundred new jobs daily. Gone are the days of needing a business loan, a building commitment, employees, and a five- to seven-year wait for profitability.

Entrepreneur magazine tells us that 68 percent of all businesses being started today require less than $10,000 to launch. Twenty-four percent require no money at all.

Brian Tracy, a nationally known sales and business consultant, says most of us have three or four ideas a year that would make us millionaires if we just did something with those ideas. But most dismiss the ideas as impractical, unrealistic, or too expensive or think that someone has probably already tried it. Thus we lose the opportunity to change our own success.

Opportunities in service businesses, telecommunications, computer and Internet options, and network marketing all provide some explosive new choices. Many of these erase the old requirements of just exchanging time for dollars. You may be accustomed to receiving $15 an hour or $31,200 a year as an exchange of *time* and *effort*. But how do you relate to the idea of using an Internet site to provide information and see the potential of bringing in $1,000 a day? Or what about a mail-order product for your gardening interest that produces hundreds of orders weekly, so that you are being compensated for *results* and not just time and effort?

Be aware of this change from a time-and-effort economy to a results-based economy. If you went into a buggy shop in 1896 and ordered a small wagon, you would not have guaranteed that

> *"Nothing splendid has ever been achieved*
> *except by those who dared believe that something*
> *inside them was superior to circumstance."*
> —*Bruce Barton*

craftsman $15 an hour or agreed that he would receive $31,200 annually. Rather, you would have agreed on a set price for the finished product—let's say $100 for a finished wagon. Now, whether it took that craftsman fifteen hours or 200 hours was not your concern; you simply paid for the completed wagon. This is a model based on results, not time and effort. What we are seeing in our current work environment is a healthy return to that simple model.

It may be necessary or advantageous for you to consider the unusual or unique as you explore new work opportunities. You could work for a sign company and be paid $20 an hour. But would you be willing to work for that same sign company and be paid $6 for every real estate sign you could paint this week? Or what about mowing yards at $65 each? Or advertising a family recipe in the back of a cooking magazine where you receive $3 for each order? Or writing an eBook on creating your own mastermind group that you sell for $17. If you are willing to look at new models, it will greatly expand opportunities for you.

(For articles on nontraditional work, and to participate in our idea sharing community, check out the action at www.48Days.net.)

Successful Nontraditional Businesses

Franchises

This is still one of the hottest forms of new business. For a franchise fee, you can purchase a proven concept for your business. Success rates are very high. You typically pay a percentage of all revenues as a franchise "royalty." Franchises range from expensive ($500,000) to very inexpensive ($595). This is not only for McDonald's or Subway. There are franchises for every concept you can imagine. A client of mine recently purchased a $10,000 cruise franchise that he and his wife operate out of their home. In the first ninety days, they booked over $100,000 in cruise packages, netting them 16 percent or $16,000. With that they recaptured all their initial expenses and began a very profitable and enjoyable self-owned business. (Check out the options at www.franchise.com or www.franchisehandbook.com/index.asp.)

Business Opportunities

These are another form of purchasing a concept, but they are not as heavily regulated as franchises, so do enough checking to feel comfortable with your choice. You get a proven model for the business, usually a start-up manual, and some initial help from the parent company. From then on you are on your own but do not have to pay any ongoing monthly royalties like with a franchise. Business opportunities you may have heard of are Merry Maids, Merle Norman Cosmetics, Liberty Tax Services, ServiceMaster, and Furniture Medic. For more information, pick up magazines like *Entrepreneur, Business Start-Ups,* and many others. Browse through them at your local grocery store. Don't assume all these ideas are scams or rip-offs. You learn by gathering lots of information. Then you can recognize an idea that is valid and fits you.

Licensing

You can sell NASCAR model cars, and Taylor Swift or Blake Shelton T-shirts, but you'll need to pay a licensing fee for using a well-known name. However, you get to use the marketing power of a recognized name for a faster start. If you are simply purchasing shirts, mugs, banners, and so forth from an established manufacturer, the licensing issue has already been addressed and you can just focus on ways to generate sales.

Distributorships

These are usually received just by asking the manufacturer or publishing company. For example, I'm a distributor for several publishing companies. I purchase their book titles at a 50 percent discount and also look for overruns and remainders in books that I can purchase at deep discounts of 90 to 95 percent, to increase my margins. If you like garden tools, sports equipment, golf accessories, or pet products, you can often just ask for the distributor agreement.

Home-Based Businesses

You may initially purchase a small inventory and be provided a little training, but for the most part you are on your own. The positives are that the cost is usually very low and you have no ongoing fees to the company that you purchased from. See an example at www.smcorp.com.

And here are some more ideas for things you can do on your own:

- Accounting
- Wedding planning
- Personal servicing
- Care for senior citizens
- Portrait painting
- Wedding photography
- Graphic design
- Computer consulting
- Making gift baskets
- Newsletter writing
- Delivery servicing
- Interior decorating
- Flea market vending
- Landscape designing
- Home inspecting
- Ceiling fans
- Import/export brokering
- House painting
- Auto detailing
- Selling used cars
- Glass tinting
- Child security systems
- Power washing
- Nutrition counseling
- Growing wild herbs
- One-person performing
- Catering
- Organic gardening
- Tour guide
- Tree removal
- Chimney cleaning
- Building decks
- Home schooling counseling
- Manners instructing
- Balloon vending
- Pet sitting
- Real estate photography
- Aerial photography
- Designing how-to brochures

Add your own ideas to this list. Search the back classified ads in magazines like *Entrepreneur, Business Start-Ups, Income Opportunities,* and more.

Intellectual Property Businesses

One of the most popular forms of business today is the promotion of intellectual property—personal development, how-to, and ways to unleash creativity and make money. Coaching, speaking, and writing are opening doors for real business income for more and more people. Many of the 48Days.net members are using intellectual property to provide the meaningful and profitable work they love.

Frequently Asked Business Start-Up Questions

1. *What is the attraction to start-up entrepreneurial businesses?* More and more people are looking for greater control of their destinies and for the chance to apply personal skills to earn income. Most people are not as interested in material wealth as they are in time freedom. More than 800,000 Americans are starting their own businesses each year, and that annual number is growing.

2. *What are the key ingredients for success?* The ability to plan, organize, and communicate. And remember, 85 percent of your success will originate from your people skills—attitude, enthusiasm, self-discipline—and only 15 percent will be due to your technical skills.

3. *Don't most new businesses fail?* Once upon a time, someone churned out the statistic that four out of five small businesses fail in their first five years of operation. No one can trace the source of this mysterious figure, and not only is it illogical but also totally untrue. Currently, we are gathering new information that helps us understand the information about businesses staying in business. Knowing the characteristics of entrepreneurs, we know they often simply choose to discontinue one business and go on to a new one. That doesn't mean the old business was not successful or profitable; they just chose to go on to a new venture.

4. *Will we really see more and more small businesses?* Many of you have already experienced the downsizing of large corporations. IBM, General Motors, and other American standards have cut their workforces dramatically. The good news is that in the last ten years, small business has accounted for 80 percent of the nation's new job growth, now adding more than three million new jobs each year. Small businesses employ 54 percent of the American workforce. What we are seeing is a healthy return to the kind of business that our country was founded on.

5. *Are there any new ideas left?* Experts estimate that more than 85 percent of the products and services that we use today will be obsolete in five years. The airplane, artificial heart valve, soft contact lens, smart phone, and Google Glass were all new ideas in past years. With the changes we are experiencing in today's market, there are thousands of opportunities for new ideas. Look at what has happened with iPhone apps and Twitter in the last few years. Ten years ago no one would have been able to foresee those opportunities.

6. *What if I'm not creative?* You don't have to be original to be successful in business. If you can do something 10 percent better than it is currently being done or provide added value, you can be wildly successful. When Domino's got into the pizza business, they didn't make better or cheaper pizza; they simply added delivery to a very common product. Meeting the desire for speed and convenience, Domino's created millionaires all across the country. Also, know that creativity is not a function of intelligence; rather it is a function of imagination. Have you ever known a child to not be imaginative? So are you. You may just need to tap into that child-like part of yourself once again.

7. *If I share my idea, will someone steal it?* Ideas are a dime a dozen. It's not even the quality of the idea but rather the quality of *the action plan* brought to that idea that determines success. Share your idea with others and get their input. Try your idea on friends and family. Make a prototype and see if people will buy it. Then gear up for a business supporting that idea. There is more to risk by not sharing your idea and getting input than there is in the slim

chance that someone will steal your idea. Everyone is very busy with their own lives. It takes a lot of time and work to launch any idea. You are probably the only person with enough desire and ambition to actually carry it through.

8. *Should I buy a franchise, distributorship, or business opportunity?* The attraction of these options is that they are a tried system for a business concept. Normally, that means a proven track to run on, marketing support, and name recognition. But buyer beware: make sure you research carefully, so you don't overpay for something you could do yourself.

9. *Where can I find the money to start a business?* With the move toward knowledge and information based businesses rather than traditional bricks and mortar, it has never been easier to start a business with little or no money. The last business I started I put $1,000 in for beginning incidentals and took it back out after the first month's profits were in. Sixty-eight percent of all new businesses being started require less than $10,000. Approximately 24 percent require zero capital. (See http://www.48Days.com/48-business-ideas for more no- or low-cost ideas.)

10. *Is there one characteristic that is central to business success?* Yes, the ability to sell. Where there is no ability to sell, even the finest product or service business will fail. Fortunately, in today's marketplace, that does not mean you have to become a Donald Trump or Mark Cuban to be successful. You can match the selling model with what you know about yourself. You can develop a method of selling that may never require you to talk to a customer, but you must have a system for selling or you will not survive.

Countdown to Work I Love

1. What do you think of when you hear the term *entrepreneur?*
2. Do you have what it takes to be on your own?
3. What service or product could you promote?
4. What invention could you develop?
5. What are three or four ideas you have had over the years that you have on the back burner or have since seen someone else develop?

6. Describe three or four times in your own work experience when you have been paid on *results* or on completion of the job rather than just for putting in your *time*.

7. What would prevent you from doing something on your own?

8. Is it exciting or frightening to think about being your own boss?

Check www.48Days.com/worksheets for more examples of new opportunities.

Chapter 12

Dream, Plan, and Act

One day, the mother of future Microsoft mogul Bill Gates walked in on her young son to find him sitting there doing nothing. She asked Bill what he was doing. "I'm thinking, Mom, I'm thinking."
—WALTER ISAACSON, "IN SEARCH OF THE
REAL BILL GATES"

Often, times of change can help us see new opportunities. Joanne and I recently moved to a new place in the country. We love the quiet, the solitude, and the natural surroundings. However, we discovered that part of those natural surroundings includes nightly visits from a couple of skunks that took up residence under our house. Their chosen gift for us was a stench that came close to prompting us to visit the local Hampton Inn. Upon researching options to see who was going to remain occupants of the house, we were referred to "All Paws," a business run by a young man named John who removes any pawed animal. John came to our house and set the traps up to transport our little friends to a new home. And then by creating some wire mesh obstacles, he discouraged the little rascals from hanging around anymore. (Incidentally, John is a musician with a well-known country singer. This is just his means of making consistent income.)

What a novel business idea! John sets the traps up for $55 and then collects another $50 for every animal trapped and removed. He told me he normally has fifteen to twenty traps set, collects four to five animals and he's finished by 9:00 a.m. You can probably do the math on that. If he had a job paying $15 an hour he would have to put in approximately sixty-five hours a week to duplicate this income. Obviously, that wouldn't leave much time for guitar playing. As with most great business ideas, this is not new and revolutionary. It's a simple idea but done by someone who just did something!

The Times, They Are A-Changin'

Back in 1970, Alvin Toffler wrote the popular book *Future Shock*, the landmark work about the effects of change on society. Toffler predicted that "millions of ordinary, psychologically normal people will face an abrupt collision with the future . . . many of them will find it increasingly painful to keep up with the incessant demand for change that characterizes our time. For them, the future will have arrived too soon."[1]

Toffler's predictions have been strikingly accurate. Peter Drucker predicted that the forty-year period (from 1970 to 2010) would bring more change than the world had ever seen. In looking back, I think we could agree with that prediction. And as we are beyond the forty-year period of change we are seeing that speed of change increase. We are rapidly approaching the time when 50 percent of all jobs will be contract, contingency labor, or one of the other models mentioned in previous chapters. These are not the characteristics of the workplace we were led to expect by our parents and grandparents.

Instead, millions of Americans have found this new future shocking and unexpected. This giant tidal wave of change has swept over our lives, frequently taking us not *toward* our dreams but setting us *back*, sometimes painfully. Rather than the pleasant retirement we anticipated at age sixty-two, we have been confronted with downsizing, outsourcing, reengineering, mergers, acquisitions, and restructuring. Seniority is no longer valued and

> *"Why is it that only a minority of our population love their work? If you are creative enough to select the ideal vocation, you can win, win big time. The really brilliant millionaires are those who selected a vocation that they love—one that has few competitors but generates high profits."*
> —*Thomas Stanley, in* **The Millionaire Mind**

common benefits like health insurance are disappearing, even in the jobs that do remain.

Seizing the Opportunities

And yet, the world has always known change. At one point in American history, approximately 79 percent of our country's workers were directly involved in the production of agriculture. Today that number is less than 3 percent. Where have the other 76 percent gone? When an Eli Whitney invents the cotton gin, where do the farm workers who have been replaced go? When a robot replaces sixteen men on an assembly line, where do these workers go? When all the employees in your company are replaced by workers somewhere else in the world at half the cost, is your future totally bleak? Are you really displaced to unemployment or an unfulfilling life, or can that displacement stimulate a transition to a higher, more fulfilling level of success?

We have seen these changes and transformations as we have moved from the agricultural age to the industrial age to the technological age and now the age of service and information. With each change, there are the seeds of new opportunities. That's one of the basic tenets of Napoleon Hill's classic book *Think and Grow Rich:* "Every adversity brings with it the seed of an equivalent advantage."[2]

Like always before in our history, we need creative people to see the needs, to see the opportunities instead of the obstacles, and to create the future. It's bad enough for the common person to be confused, but surely those of us with spiritual insight and principles at our disposal should have more clarity of direction. And yet we know that today, like at every stage of our country's development, the best opportunities may not look like those of yesterday. Today's best opportunities may not include punching a clock, having a company car, or being provided health insurance and a retirement plan. They may not involve an 8-to-5 schedule or even the need to go to an office.

> *"He who rejects change is the architect of decay. The only human institution which rejects progress is the cemetery."*
> —*Harold Wilson*

Stretching Your Thinking

Many times in exploring new directions, we are limited by our past experience. We tend to see boundaries that may not actually exist.

Here are a few mindteasers to help you think in unexpected ways (see answers at end of chapter):

- A bus with fifteen passengers crashed and all but nine people were killed. How many survivors were there?
- How many animals of each species did Moses take on the ark?
- I have two coins that total $.35 in value. One is not a quarter. What are the two coins?
- Mr. Jones was driving along the thruway with his son in the front seat. The road was icy. When Mr. Jones rounded a curve, his car skidded and rammed into a telephone pole. Mr. Jones was unhurt, but the boy broke several ribs. An ambulance took the boy to the nearest hospital. He was wheeled into the emergency operating room. The surgeon took one look at the patient and said, "I can't operate on this boy. He's my son!" How could this be?

> *"Show me a thoroughly satisfied man and I will show you a failure. I believe that restlessness is discontent, and discontent is merely the first necessity of progress." —Thomas Edison*

 Sitting for Ideas

Henry Ford once said he didn't want executives who had to work all the time. He insisted that those who were always in a flurry of activity at their desks were not being the most productive. He wanted people who would clear their desks, prop their feet up, and dream some fresh dreams. His philosophy was that only he who has the luxury of time can originate a creative thought.

Wow! When's the last time your boss told you to quit working and do more dreaming? Unfortunately, our culture glamorizes being under pressure. Having too much to do with too little time is a badge of success. Or is it?

The apostle Paul took long walks between cities, using the time to think and talk. Andrew Carnegie would go into an empty room for hours at a time as he was "sitting for ideas."

Thoreau wandered through the woods around Walden Pond, recognizing that the free time created fertile ground for original thinking. I grew up on a farm in Ohio where we got up at dawn and went to bed sometime after sunset.

A change in the weather could create an unexpected time of leisure or dreaming. Neighbors had time to sit and talk and get to any appointments "directly," which could be in ten minutes or a couple of hours.

> If you are feeling stuck, your solution may not be in doing more, but in taking a break from the busyness of life. Try a little "sitting for ideas."

You really can love your work, but that may mean taking an active part in *creating* the work you love, rather than just looking around to see what jobs are available. Seizing new opportunities and responding to unwelcome change does not require settling for less. You can have a life full of adventure and satisfaction. Russian writer Maxim Gorky said, "When work is a pleasure, life is a joy! When work is a duty, life is slavery."[3] Our work satisfaction impacts our life satisfaction. Happiness is loving what you do and knowing it is making a difference. If your life is not a joy, maybe it's time to look at some new options.

> *"Learn to pause*
> *. . . or nothing*
> *worthwhile will*
> *catch up to you."*
> *—Doug King, poet*

Joyce was frustrated in her work in medical sales. Five years earlier, she had invested all her money in opening a specialty bakery shop. Her unusual creations found immediate acceptance, and the customers flocked in as media coverage reached national business magazines. Eight months later she was bankrupt. Although people loved her tasty and appealing products, the details of running the business, complete with leases, sign permits, employees, and equipment purchases, proved to be too overwhelming. But that sense of "having something of my own" would not go away. Today Joyce has a small hot dog cart that she and her son operate. The entire purchase price was $3,800. She has exclusive rights to set up in front of the local Home Depot store on Fridays through Sundays. Joyce and her son enjoy the interaction with the many repeat retail and employee customers and take home a clear profit of approximately $1,500 each weekend. She still has her job in medical sales. The solution was not an either/or but rather one of combining the benefits of both.

 ## But He Doesn't Have a College Degree

Recently I met with my landscaper (Noe) to plan out our spring plantings and yard treatment. And then he gave me an update on the little side business he started back in his hometown in Mexico. Six years ago he told me he wanted to come up with something for his dad to do—so Dad would not just be totally dependent on his son's income. Noe bought three or four freezers from Home Depot here in Franklin, Tennessee, drove to Mexico and placed them in little markets there. Then they would fill those freezers with Popsicles they made. The markets paid nothing up front—but simply passed on 60 percent of all money generated from sales of the Popsicles—keeping 40 percent. That model proved to work very well.

Yes, people told him it would not work. Yes, well-meaning friends said he was crazy to try to do this. They told him he would have trouble finding people to work and the merchants would cheat him. But Noe forged ahead—treating people with respect and expecting the same. No, he doesn't have a business degree—in fact, he completed the sixth grade and moved into running his own businesses.

Today he has 820 freezers in place, with a goal of getting to a thousand in the next few months. He purchased a machine that can produce ten thousand Popsicles every eight hours. Currently, he is selling about nine thousand daily at the equivalent of $.70 each. He brought his cousin in to run the business there while he continues to operate his successful landscaping business here. He never borrowed a penny and attends seminars to learn how to do business better.

Obviously, this is not a high-tech business. Noe still has a flip phone and doesn't text or use Twitter, Facebook, or LinkedIn. He just provides a good product at a fair price and keeps hustling to grow his business. He never waited for someone to give him a job or to guarantee him a salary and benefits. He simply saw opportunities and took action.

What's holding you back from doing something similar? Noe had a lot of reasons for not being successful. But he took what others saw as disadvantages and moved toward success anyway. What opportunities have you seen that would open the door to this kind of success?

The Changing Face of "Business"

I operate a "virtual store" for the 48 Days products. We have no physical location, no building lease, no sign permits, no employees, and no hours of operation. Customers visit our "store" 168 hours a week and are free to browse while I am sleeping, traveling with my wife, or playing with my grandchildren. As a matter of fact, I tell people frequently that I'm quite fond of SWISS dollars—that's Sales While I Sleep Soundly.

Every morning I take a quick look at the deposits that have been made into my bank account since I went to bed the night before. I don't have to be concerned about opening the store or whether there is one person, fifty, or none in the store. I have no electric bill and don't need to make repairs to the shelves or walkways. I have no landlord and don't need to worry about bad weather conditions or street construction slowing sales. And while a traditional bookstore has about a five-mile radius of customers, I have weekly customers in every state in the country as well as from hundreds of cities around the world.

I only need a tiny fraction of the purchases of the potential market to do very well, while traditional bookstores are struggling more and more. Over 50 percent of the products I deliver are received electronically. I have no printing costs, no packaging, and no shipping charges. This is not a matter of right or wrong, good or bad; it's just a different way of doing business. Feel free to browse any time. Go ahead; you won't disturb me at all at www.48Days.com/store.

Incidentally, we do ship lots of real books and CDs every day. Those are handled by my daughter on her own schedule. She is not an "employee"—rather I am one customer for her service business. She pulls the orders from the Internet, packages the products, prints the UPS or FedEx labels, and sets them aside for the daily pickup. If she needs to take a break to address the needs of her husband and three daughters, there is no time clock to check out, no boss to ask, and no interference with attending to her many activities as a busy wife and mom. She frequently works in the same clothes she just wore to a child's birthday party, attending to our customers with care and consideration, but without the added expense or necessity of a fancy wardrobe. She spends no time commuting and has the liberty of working at 10:00 p.m. or 7:00 a.m. My business has grown dramatically through this kind of "strategic alliance" with professional service providers, who are located here in my community and around the country. It's a new way of doing business for all of us.

High-Tech Fosters High-Touch Opportunities

As creative, compassionate, and responsive people, we can increase in understanding and appreciation of new ideas, of other people, and of the world in general. A creative approach unlocks the mind and makes the spirit soar. God gives us creativity and ingenuity to make us feel *alive*. We should be leaders, not victims, as the world becomes more complex and our societal problems become increasingly difficult to solve.

Our schools, families, churches, and communities are presenting us with critical new concerns that require new solutions. Many of these issues are suffering from a lack of originality, and they need the creativity and spiritual insight of every responsible person. The solutions are not likely to be more information and more technology, but solutions that can only come from human touch and spiritual sensitivity.

Even in the career arena, you don't have to be a technological genius to survive and prosper. The U. S. Bureau of Labor Statistics forecasts 50 million new jobs opening up in the next five years with an explosion of opportunities for people who are *peacemakers, storytellers,* and *healers.* Fourteen of the thirty fastest-growing jobs in the next decade are for healers—and these are not only physicians and registered nurses. The number of certified massage therapists has quadrupled in the last ten years as the 77 million baby boomers suffer an increasing burden of minor aches and tensions. The need for counseling therapists will grow dramatically as depression and major life changes confront these people entering the second half of their lives.

Universally, people are expressing more interest in spiritual matters, giving rise for directors of religious activities and education. More than a hundred thousand new jobs for clergy and religious directors are expected in the next ten years.

The demand for simpler, more humane ways of resolving disputes will expand the opportunities for dispute mediation and arbitration. Ten years ago, there were about a hundred and fifty dispute mediation centers nationwide; today, there are at least five hundred.

Myron began attending a weekly career seminar I was offering in Nashville, Tennessee. After several weeks he approached me

> *"If God has gifted you to tell a good story, write a good book, or direct a good play, there will be opportunities for you. You can't use up creativity. The more you use, the more you have. Sadly, too often creativity is smothered rather than nurtured. There has to be a climate in which new ways of thinking, perceiving, questioning are encouraged."* —Maya Angelou

with his frustration of feeling trapped and limited. He did not have a college degree and was stuck doing the only thing he had ever done—construction work. He was bored and tired of just working for someone else. He asked about going back to school to get computer training as he viewed that as an area of opportunity. When I questioned him about special areas of competence or enjoyment even in construction, he mentioned one thing that he did find enjoyable—a new process for stamping concrete to make it look like carefully laid stones. I asked him to come out to my house the next week.

When Myron arrived, I showed him an area where I wanted a curving sidewalk that came to our front door. I wanted a five-foot-wide walk to curve around our planned waterfall. He got excited about solving every situation I presented and about how the finished product would look. Based on his excitement, I committed on the spot to have him do the job. As he had no start-up capital, I gave him half the money in advance for his initial materials. He worked hard in the creation of a beautiful curving walkway that immediately generated comments from clients and friends at our house.

From that simple start we were able to refer him to several additional friends and they did the same. He decided on the name, Lasting Impressions, and went on to generate well over $100,000 in sales in his first year of business. It's his business, he's doing what he loves, and it draws from all those years of working when he thought he was only making a living.

In the last few years I have seen a lady who personalizes candy bar wrappers, a young man who picks up dry cleaning from businesses, a couple who cut up flawed fabric into commercial rags, a

> *"What I lack is to be clear in my mind what
> I am to do, not what I am to know. . . . The thing
> is to understand myself, to see what God really
> wishes me to do. . . . To find the idea for which
> I can live and die." —Søren Kierkegaard*

fireman who services cologne vending machines on his off days, a guy who buys discontinued cameras in bulk and then sells them individually on eBay, a gal who carved the amazing eagle out of a dead tree on our property, and a lady who makes great cheese-cakes for local restaurants. All of these people are experiencing time freedom and levels of income only hoped for by most people. And yet these great business ideas are not new and revolutionary. They are simple but done by someone who just did something! A good idea will not put money in anybody's pocket, but combined with a plan of action that good idea can give you time control and unlimited income. For a business-planning guide, see our list of resources at www.48Days.com/worksheets.

Wrap Up and Launch

Don't look at any circumstances or past history with regret, but simply learn from them as you create a clear plan for the future. Everyone has events that have helped to make us who and what we are. You simply must look at where you are and then cre-ate a clear plan for the future you want. That process of seeing five years out and clarifying what you want that to be will immediately begin to lessen the uncertainty about any current situation.

As has been stated repeatedly, this is a very individualized process. Clarify what unique characteristics you bring to the table. Even when confronted with the realities of making a living, you still are not locked into repeating what you have done. God has equipped you with unique skills. Sort out the positives and expect to find applications that draw on your known abilities but also address the mission of your life. We want options that complement your multiple life goals—going beyond just job or career.

Understand your areas of strength and how they impact orga-nizational focus and leadership. If you have great financial and administrative abilities, those should be explored as you look at possible new alternatives. If you have the ability to organize, plan, develop systems, and self-start projects, then embrace those in the selection process. Recognizing competence in technical, analyti-cal, and detail skills can be integrated even if you are creating your own business. Those characteristics will help you create a sales/ marketing model for your business that does not depend on nose-to-nose selling but, rather, on established systems. Your enjoyment of church involvement, your passion for photography, your desire to increase your income, and your desire to contribute to worthy and noble causes can all be considerations in identifying a new direction. (Remember Eric Liddle in *Chariots of Fire*—"God made me fast, and when I run I feel His pleasure.") Don't think this is a time to ignore your true passions even if the normal applications do not seem to produce the income results. And remember the story of the ten talents. If you have the ability to increase your responsibilities and income and channel it wisely, then not doing so may be poor stewardship. Your desire to help, to serve people, to do something that lasts in people's lives, and to make a difference will all help in selecting the proper direction.

As I often relate, the eagles build a nest using thorn-bush strands to lock it together. Then they cover those thorns with leaves and feathers to make the nest soft and comfortable. However, when the little eaglets are about twelve weeks old, the mom and dad eagles begin to remove the protection from the thorns. Pretty soon the little eaglets are up on the edge of the nest to avoid the pain and discomfort. Then the mom and dad eagle fly by with tasty morsels of food just out of reach. The little eaglet sees that if he leaves the nest, he'll drop and crash on the rocks below. However, as the discomfort continues the little eaglet finally decides even the risk of the crash below can't be worse than the pain and hunger he's feeling. And of course you know what happens. Rather than crashing on the rocks, the little eagle discovers he can fly—and he experiences a level of success beyond what he could have imagined. It just required taking that big step of faith. I believe that God sometimes allows circumstances in our lives, not to leave us in pain and hunger but to lead us to higher levels of success that we would not otherwise explore. See the thorns in your situation as a prod to explore new options.

I love the symbolic characteristics of eagles. They are powerful, distinctive animals. Able to soar above the rest of the world, as

> *"Make no little plans; they have no magic*
> *to stir men's souls and themselves will*
> *not be realized. Make big plans; aim high in*
> *hope and work, remembering that a noble,*
> *logical diagram once recorded will not die."*
> —*Daniel Burnham, Chicago architect*

adults they could easily become content, unfocused, and lazy. And yet, they instinctively realize that to maintain pure survival, they must be aware and take the initiative for new methods, strategies, and information. We, as well, must follow their lead.

In today's rapidly changing environment, lack of growth or contentment with the status quo will put a person in jeopardy—and likely in pain and hunger. Companies, individuals, and even churches that are not looking for innovative ways to do things are being left behind.

We are in the age of the knowledge worker where new learning is essential. Keep learning; don't end your education when you finish school. Degrees and training received ten years ago may not be relevant today. Industries and technology that previously took forty to fifty years to become outdated are now becoming obsolete in four to five years. Computers are replacing people, information is replacing technology, and results are replacing time and effort. Constant growth is an absolute requirement for simply maintaining a valued place in today's world.

Change is inevitable; how will you respond? You can choose to wring your hands as a victim, or use your God-given creativity to see where He is leading you. Each of us has been given unique skills, abilities, personality tendencies, values, dreams, and passions. We should be at the forefront as innovators and inventors, shining examples of excellence and accomplishment in all we do. Creating an individual path of mission and calling, we cannot then be victimized by any corporate downsizing or any other effects of the changing workplace. Rather, we will seize the opportunities and lead the way to higher levels of fulfillment, income, and methods for blessing those around us.

After considering your best options, you are ready to create your own 48-Day plan! Check out all the resources at www.48Days.com for additional help, and updated resources and then begin to work through the stages of your plan. You can do this. *You can achieve the success you are seeking.* Take inventory, focus, create a plan, and act.

Countdown to Work I Love

1. What action can you take in the next 48 Days to put you on the path for what you want to accomplish?

2. What idea have you gotten while on the beach or mowing your yard that could be worth more than a lifetime of hard work?

3. What seeds did you plant in your mind five years ago that brought you to where you are today?

4. What unique skills do you have that may be the basis for a creative business (writing, drawing, building, analyzing, singing, driving, thinking, etc.)?

5. Do you have any ideas that would fall into the "peacemakers, storytellers, and healers" category?

6. Can you think of an idea that would create SWISS dollars for you?

7. Do you ever give yourself time to "sit for ideas"?

8. How does your culture, environment, and experience perhaps limit your being able to see new opportunities?

Answers to "Stretching Your Thinking"

- All but nine people were killed; thus there were nine survivors—not six!
- How many of each species did Moses take on the ark? Check your Bible. It wasn't Moses; it was Noah!
- The two coins are a dime and a quarter. Yes, I said one is not a quarter, and that's true: one is a dime, not a quarter.
- The surgeon was the little boy's mother. Our assumption is that a surgeon is a man.

Appendix

These resources and more can be found at www.48Days.com/
worksheets.

- 48 Days Schedule—From Day 1 to Day 48
- Sample Résumés
- Sample Introduction Letter
- Sample Cover Letter
- Sample Follow-Up Letter
- Worksheets for Exercises Listed
- Helpful Internet Sites for Job-Hunting
- Helpful Internet Sites for Small Businesses
- Helpful Internet Sites for Women
- College-Related Internet Sites
- Access to Facilitator Information
- Overview of Six-Week 48 Days Seminar
- Suggested Reading List (Send e-mail to Reading@48Days.
  com)

Notes

Chapter 1

1. Oxford Dictionaries.com, "work," accessed June 9, 2014, http://www.oxforddictionaries.com/us/definition/american_english/work?q=work.
2. Merriam-webster.com, "leisure," accessed June 11, 2014, http://www.merriam-webster.com/dictionary/leisure.
3. Merriam-webster.com, "retire," accessed June 11, 2014, http://www.merriam-webster.com/dictionary/retire.
4. Thomas Stanley, *The Millionaire Mind* (Kansas City, MO: Andrews McMeel Publishing, 2001), 186.
5. Merriam-webster.com, "spiritual," accessed June 11, 2014, http://www.merriam-webster.com/dictionary/spiritual.
6. Richard Foster, *Prayer: Finding the Heart's True Home* (New York: Harper One, 2002), 158.
7. Kahlil Gibran, *The Prophet* (New York: Alfred A. Knopf, Inc., 1923), 28.
8. A. H. Maslow, (1943). A theory of human motivation. *Psychological Review, 50*(4), 370–96. Retrieved from http://psychclassics.yorku.ca/Maslow/motivation.htm.

Chapter 2

1. Dale Carnegie, *How to Win Friends and Influence People* (New York: Simon and Schuster, 1936), 103.
2. Robert J. Kriegel, *If It Ain't Broke . . . Break It! and Other Unconventional Wisdom for a Changing Business World* (Little, Brown & Company: 1991), 187.
3. As quoted in William S. Walsh, *International Encyclopedia of Prose and Poetical Quotations* (1951), 85.

4. As quoted from The Napoleon Hill Foundation (http://www.naphill.org/posts/tftd/thought-for-the-day-friday-august-17-2012).

5. As quoted in Successories Douglas MacArthur Quotes (http://www.successories.com/iquote/author/1713/douglas-macarthur-quotes/2).

6. Hannah More quoted by Robert Allen, *Multiple Streams of Income* (Hoboken, NJ: John Wiley & Sons, Inc., 2000), 174.

7. Viktor Frankl, *Man's Search for Meaning* (New York: Washington Square Press Publication, 1959), 86–87.

Chapter 3

1. Dictionary.com, "education," accessed May 30, 2014, http://dictionary.reference.com/browse/education?s=t.

2. Earl Nightingale, *The Strangest Secret*, first recorded in 1956, http://www.nightingale.com/products/strangest-secret.

3. See http://www.searchquotes.com/quotation/The_man_who_is_too_old_to_learn_was_probably_always_too_old_to_learn./400879.

4. See http://www.nextbigwhat.com/sir-ken-robinson-on-creativity-297/TED video.

5. See http://www.henry-ford.net/english/quotes.html.

6. Joseph A. Schumpeter, *Capitalism, Socialism and Democracy* (London and New York: Routledge, 1943), 152.

7. Sir Ken Robinson, Bring on the Learning Revolution!, TED talk, February 2010, video. See http://www.ted.com/talks/sir_ken_robinson_bring_on_the_revolution.

8. See http://www.nytimes.com/2009/05/24/magazine/24labor-t.html?pagewanted=all&_r=0. Quote attributed to Alan Binder, accessed June 14, 2014.

Chapter 4

1. See http://thinkexist.com/quotation/there_are_certain_things_that_are_fundamental_to/346905.html.

2. See http://dictionary.reference.com/browse/vocation.

3. Thomas Merton, *New Seeds of Contemplation* (New York: New Directions Publishing Company, 1961), 29.

4. See http://www.searchquotes.com/quotation/Where_the_spirit_does_not_work_with_the_hand_there_is_no_art/11638/

5. See Dictionary.com, accessed June 14, 2014, http://dictionary.reference.com/browse/career?s=t.

6. Accessed June 14, 2014, http://dictionary.reference.com/browse/job?s=t.

7. See http://en.wikipedia.org/wiki/Avodah.

8. Irving Stone, quoted in Pat Williams and Jim Denny, *Go for the Magic* (Nashville: Thomas Nelson, 1995), 175–76.

Chapter 5

1. See http://frederickbuechner.me/content/place-where-god-calls-you.
2. See http://www.appleseeds.org/rohn_face-enemy.htm.
3. Napoleon Hill, *Think and Grow Rich* (Meriden, CT: The Ralston Society, 1944), 327.
4. James Allen, *As a Man Thinketh*, essay originally published 1903, public domain.
5. Peter Drucker, *Drucker on Asia* (Oxford: Butterworth-Heinemann 1997), 186.
6. See http://www.people.com/people/archive/article/0,,20133675,00.html, accessed June 11, 2014.

Chapter 6

1. See https://www.walden.org/Library/Quotations/The_Henry_D._Thoreau_Mis-Quotation_Page, accessed June 14, 2014.
2. See http://www.emersoncentral.com/selfreliance.htm, accessed June 14, 2014.
3. Laurence F. Peter, *The Peter Principle* (New York: William Morrow & Company, Inc., 1969), 27.
4. See http://www.social-sciences-and-humanities.com/PDF/seven_pillars_of_wisdom.pdf, accessed June 14, 2014.

Chapter 7

1. See http://www.nytimes.com/2007/01/03/technology/03google.html?pagewanted=all&_r=0, accessed June 14, 2014.

Chapter 8

1. As quoted in Fast Company, Richard Bolles, *What Color Is Your Parachute?* (New York: Ten Speed Press, 2002), http://www.fastcompany.com/46653/all-right-moves-dont-lose-hope.
2. As quoted in ABC News, Losing Your Job Can Make You Sick, http://abcnews.go.com/Business/story?id=86928.

Chapter 9

1. See http://www.careerbuilder.com/jobposter/small-business/article.aspx?articleid=ATL_0174INTERVIEWBLUNDERS.
2. Bob Goff, *Love Does* (Nashville: Thomas Nelson, 2012), 204–5.

3. David J. Schwartz, *The Magic of Thinking Big* (Cornerstone Library, 1979), 51.

Chapter 10

1. Jonathan Swift, *The Works of the Rev. Jonathan Swift, D.D.,* (John Nicols, F.A.S. Edinburgh & Perth, 1803), 86.
2. Thomas Stanley, *The Millionaire Mind* (Kansas City, MO: Andrews McMeel Publishing, 2000), 10.

Chapter 11

1. Daniel Goleman, *Emotional Intelligence* (New York: A Bantam Book, 1995), 34.

Chapter 12

1. Alvin Toffler, *Future Shock* (A Bantam Book, 1971), 9.
2. Napoleon Hill, *Think and Grow Rich* (Meriden, CT: The Ralston Society, 1944), 55.
3. See http://thinkexist.com/quotation/when-work-is-a-pleasure-life-is-joy-when-work-is/535083.html, accessed June 14, 2014.

DREAM, PLAN AND ACT!

48 Days to the Work You Love came out of my concern that people would talk about new ideas and opportunities, and yet I would see them two years later and nothing had changed in their lives. I am convinced 48 days is long enough to evaluate where you are, get the advice of people you trust, decide what your best options are, create a plan, and *ACT!*

WANT TO HEAR MORE FROM DAN MILLER?

Check out Dan's blog and sign up for weekly emails

www.48Days.com/blog

www.48Days.com/listen

48Days.NET is the **Idea Networking** site for people who are committed to finding - or creating - work that is meaningful, purposeful, and profitable. That includes entrepreneurs, artists, authors, musicians, those working from home, small business owners, BIG business owners, franchisees, independent contractors, reps...etc. as well as people who have found that fit as an employee. People who work on their own terms.

Join the *48Days.net* Community

Your Headquarters for Creating the Work You Love

Check out all of our products
www.48Days.com/store

Come see us LIVE!
www.48Days.com/LiveEvents

Our mission is to foster the process of imagining, dreaming and introspection, to help people find their calling and true path, and to translate that into meaningful, purposeful and profitable daily work...within 48 days!